AYN RAND

AYN RAND
a sense of life

THE COMPANION BOOK BY MICHAEL PAXTON

Publisher's Note

The idea to publish this book came to me while viewing an early screening of Michael Paxton's marvelous film. In January 1997 I attended the Sundance Film Festival in Park City, Utah. Parallel with Sundance there is an alternative film festival, Slamdance, also held in Park City. Mr. Paxton's film was to me the most powerful and moving film at either Sundance or Slamdance that year. Ayn Rand's passion, work, and life story were powerfully portrayed. I arranged to meet Mr. Paxton after the screening and we agreed to work together on a book that had the same visual style and narrative content of the film.

First Edition
01 00 99 98   5 4 3 2 1

This is a Peregrine Smith Book, published by
Gibbs Smith, Publisher P.O. Box 667 Layton, Utah 84041
Toll-free orders (1-800) 748-5439
Visit our Web site: www.gibbs-smith.com

Design by Pamela Fraser
Art direction/montage design by Joel Levinson
Printed in Hong Kong

For more information on how to see the film of *Ayn Rand: A Sense of Life*, please contact any of the following Web sites:
www.asenseoflife.com
www.strandrel.com (Strand Releasing)
or email: strand@strandrel.com

For information on Ayn Rand's philosophy, please contact the Ayn Rand Institute at (310) 306-9232, 4640 Admiralty Way, Suite 406, Marina del Rey, CA 90292, www.aynrand.org

Paxton, Michael
    Ayn Rand : a sense of life / Michael Paxton. — 1st ed.
       p.   cm.
"A companion book to the feature documentary."
"A Peregrine Smith book."
ISBN 0-87905-845-5
1. Rand, Ayn—Biography.   2. Women novelists, American — 20th century—Biography.
3. Women philosophers—United States—Biography.   4. Objectivisim (Philosophy) I. Title.
PS3535.A547Z82 1998
813' .52—dc21   97-47219
                                             CIP

Foreword

Ayn Rand lived a life that could have inspired one of her own novels. She not only wrote about strength and greatness; she embodied them.

When she escaped to America from the Soviet Union in 1926, Ayn Rand was an impoverished immigrant, only twenty-one years old. At last, I am in the world's freest country, she thought—and then had to endure almost two decades of bitter struggle against every kind of social and financial obstacle. But her motto was "Price no object." She went on to become a famous writer, a leading spokesman for capitalism, and a revolutionary philosopher. Today her ideas are studied in high schools and colleges around the world.

Ayn Rand, during her lifetime, would not have allowed a movie about her life to be made—for the reason given by Howard Roark, the hero of *The Fountainhead*, when Gail Wynand tells him that he (Roark) should have been the model for the statue in Roark's Stoddard Temple to the glory of Man.

> *"No," says Roark. "I'm too egotistical for that."*
> *"Egotistical?" Wynand exclaims. "An egotist would have loved it. You use words in the strangest way."*
> *"In the exact way," Roark replies. "I don't wish to be the symbol of anything. I'm only myself."*

Ayn with Leonard Peikoff in the late 1950's.

Despite this, however, I am certain—after spending thirty years as her student and friend—that Ayn Rand would not object to *me* authorizing this movie. As her future executor, I several times questioned her about her wishes in respect to her property. "What you do with my things after I'm dead," she answered, "is your concern, not mine."

My concern is and has always been to spread her ideas as best I can, using every medium and means available—limited only by the requirements of integrity and good taste. By these standards, the present movie eminently qualifies.

Ayn Rand was born into a Russian culture hostile to all of her values; Russia was hostile, above all, to her "benevolent-universe" sense of life—i.e., to her conviction, flowing from a thoroughly rational philosophy, that *the good is achievable*; that happiness, not suffering, is the normal state of man. Because this sense of life is the theme of Michael Paxton's movie, he has asked me to comment here on the role of the movies in Ayn Rand's youth, including their role in helping her to sustain the "benevolent-universe" approach.

As a child, Ayn Rand had only two windows onto the West, two arts that kept this joyous vision of life from being crushed under the Soviet reality: Viennese operetta and Western silent movies. Operetta, she has said, "was my first great art passion. It really saved my life. It was the most marvelous benevolent-universe, a shot in the arm, practically a narcotic. Only it wasn't a narcotic in the sense of escape, because it was the one positive fuel that I could have. My sense of life was kept going on that. It was a life-saving transfusion."

Later, when American and German silent movies appeared in Leningrad, she discovered that movies offered "a much more specific, not merely symbolic, view of life abroad." Thus, "movies supplanted the operettas in my life. . . . I began to see movies every night practically. That was the most wonderful period. That was one of my happiest periods as such. I don't mean in the total, but at least in this aspect, because it was almost as if I had a private avenue of seeing the world outside."

Even though Ayn Rand's chosen medium was the written word, the movies continued to play a key role in her early life, not only in Russia, but also in America.

* *She began attending movies regularly in 1922, at the age of seventeen, and remained an avid fan in America; for seven years, through 1929, she saw well over 400 movies and kept a detailed diary of every one.*

* *In 1924, she entered the State Film Institute in Leningrad, in order to qualify as a screenwriter.*

* *Her first two published works, in Russian, were about the movies: a pamphlet on Hollywood, and one on a special favorite of hers, silent screen star Pola Negri.*

* *Her first job in America was as an extra in* The King of Kings, *Cecil B. DeMille's 1926 silent epic. She had met the famous director on her first day in Hollywood, by sheer accident; later, she worked for him as a junior screen-writer. It was on the movie set in 1926 that she met her future husband, actor (later painter) Frank O'Connor.*

* *The first American sale of her writing was of a screenplay, "Red Pawn," which was purchased by Universal in 1932.*

* *Ayn Rand moved to New York City in 1934, but returned to Hollywood in 1943 to write the screenplay for* The Fountainhead.

* *During the next four years, she worked for producer Hal Wallis, for whom she wrote* Love Letters, You Came Along, *and other scripts. One of her projects in this period was a screenplay, unfortunately never produced, about the development of the atomic bomb (for details of this latter, see* Journals of Ayn Rand, *edited by David Harriman).*

By the time of her permanent move to Manhattan in 1951, Ayn Rand had become thoroughly disenchanted with Hollywood. But, much as she despised the movie industry's disintegration, she never forgot what the movies, especially certain of the Romantic silent movies, had once meant to her.

One of Ayn Rand's favorite actresses was Mia May, an Austrian silent screen star. In 1948, she wrote a thank you letter to Miss May. "I find it very difficult to tell you how grateful I am for the [publicity] pictures you sent me. I have no way to explain how much they mean to me. It is my youth brought back—or, rather, a reward for the very difficult years of my youth, when the name 'Mia May' and the things you represented were the symbol of the only beauty and relief I had while being imprisoned in hell. . . . I have had a very hard struggle to reach the things I wanted. That I should meet you in person, when I have finally broken my way into pictures, is like a special reward to me, something very personal and precious—because the kind of pictures I want to make are in the style and spirit of the pictures you made. It is a spirit which does not exist in the world any longer—and part of my battle is to bring it back."

This spirit—the factor that saved Ayn Rand through all her battles—was, in crucial part, the benevolent-universe sense of life which she experienced as one of the foundation stones of her soul, and which she always conveyed in her writings. It is that sense of life—the sense of an open universe, where achievement is possible and pain merely an ugly accident—that provides the key to this first documentary about her life.

In an age like ours—when evil is deemed to be real and virtue a mere illusion, when feet of clay, real or invented, are regarded as the essence of "objective" biography, and any positive portrait is dismissed as "hagiography"; when the upholders of the "anti-hero" compete to spew venom on anyone who defends the possibility of human stature—in an age like this, Michael Paxton has had the courage to say: "Ayn Rand is *a value*, and here is the proof."

He has also had the skill to take seemingly inadequate materials (such as still pictures, movie clips, and interviews of friends) and make them speak eloquently—much more eloquently than I thought possible.

Mr. Paxton has created a vivid testament to Ayn Rand's character and to her achievement. I hope that this movie can inspire young viewers in the same way that movies inspired Ayn Rand herself, and can broadcast to each of them the same message: "Don't give up the struggle for your values, however bad the state of the world, because success is possible—it is possible to *you*, here and now, on earth and in your lifetime."

Leonard Peikoff
Irvine, California
February 1998

Pastel portraits of Ayn Rand and Frank O'Connor by noted artist Leonebel Jacobs, 1948.

Introduction

It was a time of peace marches and violence. The sixties had exploded and ebbed. As a quiet, intense boy of thirteen, I was a "lost soul," immensely afraid of what the future held for the world and for me. Concurrently, however, I had reached a plateau of utter boredom. So little of what I had learned in school related to the real world or to the issues I was grappling with in my day-to-day life. Was the world real or only an illusion? How do we know something is true? What does it mean to be moral? And, which politics are the right politics? Although I felt a passion for learning, the answers I got from the secular and Catholic worlds were crushingly empty and pat. It was 1970, and the altruistic "everybody should love everybody" motif the culture was being bombarded with clashed with my own way of thinking. The idea that "others should come first" only prompted me to ask, "Well, who are the 'others' and why should I feel *anything* for them?" Of course, I cared about certain people in my life. But that was just it: I *chose* to care about them, and no amount of rhetoric—from the churches, temples or political platforms—could change that fact. So, what were all these organizations, groups and harbingers of altruism making such a fuss about? And, how can we love everybody? How can we love anything without being selfish? It just didn't make sense.

I fought to keep from becoming alienated, withdrawn and despondent. But somewhere under all the loneliness and frustration, there was a distant voice that nagged at my subconscious. "The world simply *has* to make sense," it kept saying through the fog. "Otherwise, how can we be here? How can there even be a 'here'?"

It was this glimmer of logical thinking—like a flame underground—that kept me at an uncomfortable level of anxiety—and hope. Somehow I believed that there were others who felt as I did. Fortunately, I was too young to be patient, and I soon reached the point where all my questions had to be answered or forever hold their peace. I had to do *something!* On one crisp fall day in Upstate New York, I was moved to act on my impatience. With more determination than hope, I walked into a local bookstore with one goal in mind: Find a book, *any* book, that makes sense! Just to read a few sentences that said something *important,* something I could believe in, something that my mind could identify as undoubtedly *true.* Nothing short of this could have saved me from eternal befuddlement.

As naive as I was in thinking that all of my questions would be answered by browsing through a bookstore, I walked down the fiction aisle and scanned the racks of colorful paperbacks. But only one book caught my eye. The cover depicted three faces surrounded by barbed wire, their expressions tortured but exalted as they struggled to be free. Twenty-seven years later, I still remember the thought that hit me with such fierce intensity: That's *exactly* how I feel! Without hesitation, I picked up the book and read the publisher's book jacket. *"This is the story of a ruthless, blazing and courageous love, a love that flung defiance against the scavengers of human souls,"* were the first words I read. *"In a bitter struggle of the individual against the collective, three people stand forth with the mark of the unconquered in the bearing. Against a vivid panorama of political revolution and personal revolt, Ayn Rand offers an answer that challenges the modern conscience."* The next thing I knew, I was standing in front of the cashier and buying that book—*We the Living* by Ayn Rand—for $2.75. My life would be changed forever.

In the years that followed, I discovered that all the questions that had been plaguing me had been addressed boldly and clearly in Ayn Rand's books and articles. From her other novels—*Anthem, The Fountainhead* and *Atlas Shrugged*—I came to appreciate the value of the human mind. From her nonfiction books, I gained a new understanding of a variety of topics—freedom, selfishness, art and, most importantly, man's place in the universe.

In 1977, I had the opportunity to see Ayn Rand speak at the Ford Hall Forum in Boston, Massachusetts. I had a seat up in the balcony, far, far away from the stage. As Ayn Rand stood at the podium—a tiny figure against the expanse of the large, empty stage—I heard her Russian accent for the first time. But soon I heard only the ingenious ideas—

ideas that I had been reading and thinking about—now being spoken out loud by the woman who had created them. Then, I watched as she fielded question after question with incredible precision and humor. No matter how rude or cantankerous the questioners became, she responded with unfailing fortitude and logic. When I left the auditorium that night, I experienced an overpowering sense of all that was right with the world and an uncompromising benevolence.

For weeks after this experience, I would awaken from dreams with an image seared into my memory: Ayn Rand's face and those large, glowing eyes. Like a warm, wise owl she seemed to be looking into my soul and challenging me to think.

Many years later, this image came back to inspire me when I had the opportunity to make a documentary film about Ayn Rand's life. As I began writing the script and gathering material to tell her story, I would always hearken back to my first impressions of her; to all that she had clarified for me through her books—like the concepts of reason, self-esteem and laissez-faire capitalism—and, in how she offered the world this knowledge—directly, passionately and *selfishly*. But as I began to flesh out the film on paper, I have to admit I became a bit downhearted. I was reminded of something Miss Rand said at the close of *The Ayn Rand Letter* (a newsletter in which she applied her philosophy to current events) in 1975. She said, "I began to feel as if I would have to become a journalist. Casting no aspersions on that once honorable and always badly needed profession, a journalist is what I most emphatically am not." So, to make a movie about Ayn Rand's life presented a dilemma to me as a filmmaker. As an artist, I wanted to do more than present her experiences or annotate her philosophic ideas on film. I had to look long and hard at the facts and then go beyond the safety of their realm to express the summation of who Ayn Rand was as a person. I had to see where my imagination could take me without ever leaving the foundation of the journalistic reality of her life.

In an interview Ayn Rand did with *Mademoiselle* magazine in 1967, she was asked, "Would you talk a bit about your early life?" and she replied, "I seldom think about my life in that sense. What interests me in a person is his ideas, not the chance events." Ayn Rand herself was certainly more than the chance events, brilliant ideas, or the achievements and values she embraced. She was all these things woven together in a tapestry rich with color, inspiration and genius. This was the key to essentializing Ayn Rand; to show how *she* saw the universe—her own personal, emotional response to existence. It was her "sense of life" that I wanted to capture—her unrelenting belief that we can succeed if we only try and that the good is possible. Hence, the theme of the feature documentary *Ayn Rand: A Sense of Life* was born. It was to be a filmed document of the "spirit" of that which had spoken to me on countless occasions: from the cover of *We the Living*, and the plots of Ayn Rand's novels and the minds of her characters, to that distant seat at the back of that auditorium where I first saw those incredible eyes looking out at the world.

Ultimately, the film took four years to complete. But it was during the researching and writing of the script that what I thought I knew about human beings was confirmed. We are creatures of *value choices*. Whatever we hold dear to our hearts and minds is what decides the path we will take. Ayn Rand was the ultimate concretization of this. Consciously valuing freedom, she left Russia for America. Wanting to communicate her values through her writing, she first wrote for the movies and then produced a stunning array of novels and nonfiction books. And, through all the ups and downs, fortune and famine, fame and obscurity, it was her consistency, ambition and hard work that have created a legacy of values. Values that celebrate the best of the human spirit, and a benevolence that used to be reserved only for the gods.

I hope this companion book allows the reader—as does the film—to experience the same world I was so fortunate to have witnessed firsthand. I also hope that, by its existence, the "lost souls" of future generations will lessen in number. And that, as the millennium approaches, those who choose to think and care about human life on earth will have their journey enriched by being exposed to what Ayn Rand had to say.

Michael Paxton
Hollywood, California
November 17, 1997

Michael Paxton discusses a scene from Ayn Rand's play Ideal *with Janne Peters (Kay Gonda).*
Photo: James Sorenson

Acknowledgements

Many people contributed and collaborated to create *Ayn Rand: A Sense of Life*. And since there would not be a companion book without there first being a film, I must thank all those who helped to tell Ayn Rand's story: Monroe Trout, Jeff Britting, Ellen Raphael, Alik Sakharov, Jim Farrell, Michael M. Moore, Cynthia Wells, Lauren Schaffer, Christopher Earl, Jeff Hoffman, Gregory Haggard, Timothy J. Borquez, Chuck Winston, Michael Keller, Joel Levinson, Stewart Margolis, Andrew Kain and Strand Releasing.

I want to thank Leonard Peikoff for trusting me with this project and for allowing me access to all of Ayn Rand's photos and private papers, Cynthia Peikoff for her thoughtful patience in approving the narration script for the film, and both of them for offering their insights and recollections on camera. Thanks to Harry Binswanger, Mike Berliner, John Ridpath, Al Ramrus, Mike Wallace and Sylvia Bokor for sharing their experiences and thoughts about Ayn Rand.

Jeff Britting is owed a great deal of credit for his organizing and researching the materials that ended up in the film and this book. He was a valuable "razor," cutting away a lot of fat before it reached me. This afforded me the time I needed to focus on writing the script and selecting only the materials that were visually interesting. He, along with Mike Berliner and Richard Ralston at the Ayn Rand Institute, and a research team across the globe, made accessing important information and the finishing of the project possible. Jeff was also the one who sat with me through *The King of Kings* at the Silent Movie Theatre in West Hollywood, hoping to find Ayn Rand in one of the crowd scenes. Not having success there, we went to the Academy of Motion Picture Arts and Sciences Library and looked through all the stills from the film. It was Jeff who found the first still that showed Ayn Rand working as an extra on that landmark film.

The only downside of reading the book instead of watching the film is that you cannot hear two of the most integral elements that make *A Sense of Life* a success: Sharon Gless's brilliant narration and Jeff Britting's moving score.

Director Michael Paxton and Cinematographer Alik Sakharov on the set of A Sense of Life.
Photo: James Sorenson

Sharon Gless made an invaluable contribution with her warm and intelligent reading of the narration. An utter joy to work with, she is a professional and passionate actress. I could not have had anyone better to interpret the words of my narration. At one session, she looked up from the script and commented on how the narration was "like music." Indeed, she was the ultimate "singer," in the most profound sense of the word. And she stayed with the project over its long journey through rough cuts and release prints, always accommodating my needs to make the final narration just right for the film. I am so proud to have worked with her and will always be her biggest fan.

Jeff is responsible for creating the original score for the film, which truly put the finishing touches on the universe I wanted to create. Despite a meager budget and an incredibly short schedule, he and Greg Haggard produced a truly inspirational soundtrack. It was with a great deal of patience that Jeff came up with a multitude of first-rate melodies and Greg achieved the proper orchestrations to underscore Ayn's story.

If you have already seen the film, I hope the memories of these essential elements—the narration and the score—will come back to move you. If you haven't yet seen the film, a wonderful experience awaits you.

Mike Berliner, aside from reading from his book *Letters of Ayn Rand* on camera, was a constant source of support and encouragement. He helped in the completion of the film and this book (including writing the captions for the photos), and was always there to fact-check *something*. He is also, as the executive director of the Ayn Rand Institute, preserving the legacy of Ayn Rand's manuscripts and papers for future generations.

I would also like to thank Roxanne Mayweather at Searchworks, who helped make up for all of my inexperience in licensing materials. I am a great lover of movies and had an unending appetite for including clips. Alas, budgetary constraints kept this to a bare minimum. Through Roxanne's patience and respect for the material we were trying to amass, we were able to complete this process. Despite our long schedule, she stuck with me to the end and has remained a good friend in the process.

I want to thank all the companies, libraries and studios that were willing to license their material to me, especially Multimedia Entertainment, Inc., for allowing me to use so much of the shows with Phil Donahue and Ayn Rand, and Mike Wallace for the use of one of the best interviews with Ayn Rand ever caught on Kinescope.

Also, much gratitude to the following for their help in bringing this book to press: Gibbs Smith, Joel Levinson, Pam Fraser, Madge Baird, Donna Montrezza and Diane LeMont.

Finally, I want to extend one absurdly inadequate "thank you" to Ayn Rand—for all she went through and for all she has given the world in the name of her own happiness. Mine is a gratitude that cannot be overstated; her ideas and the sense of life she articulated so well have become the benchmark of my own life path.

Special Thanks

to

MONROE TROUT

for his contribution to this project.

Note to the Reader

The following people were interviewed on camera for the film.
Their comments were extemporaneous and have not been edited for this book:

LEONARD PEIKOFF, Ph.D.

Ayn Rand's intellectual heir and friend for 30 years

HARRY BINSWANGER, Ph.D.

Philosophy professor and friend of Ayn Rand

MICHAEL S. BERLINER

Editor, Letters of Ayn Rand

CYNTHIA PEIKOFF

Friend and secretary of Ayn Rand

DANIEL E. GREENE

Artist

JOHN RIDPATH, Ph.D.

*Professor of economics and social science,
York University, Toronto*

SYLVIA BOKOR

Artist

AL RAMRUS

Writer-producer

MIKE WALLACE

CBS news correspondent

ALSO
"*****" signifies that the word or phrase in the narration was directly quoted from Ayn Rand

AYN RAND

A Sense of Life

WRITTEN AND DIRECTED BY

Michael Paxton

NARRATED BY

Sharon Gless

16

"If a life can have a 'theme song' – and I believe every worthwhile one has – mine is a religion, an obsession or a mania – or all of these – expressed in one word: Individualism.

"I was born with that obsession and have never seen and do not know now a cause
more worthy, more misunderstood, more seemingly hopeless and more tragically
needed." Ayn Rand, novelist and philosopher, wrote these words in 1936. "Call it fate
or irony," she wrote, "but I was born, of all countries on earth, in the one [least]
suitable for a fanatic of individualism: Russia."

"I decided to be a writer at the age of nine, and everything I have done was
integrated to that purpose. I am an American by choice and conviction. I was born in
Europe, but I came to America because this was the country where one could be fully
free to write."

Ayn Rand developed the theory that everyone has a subconscious view of the universe and man's place in it. It is a person's most personal, emotional response to existence, and what she termed a "sense of life."

The Mike Wallace Interview (1959)

MIKE WALLACE

And now to our story. Down through history, various political and philosophical movements have sprung up, but most of them have died. Some, however, like democracy or communism, take hold and affect the entire world. Here, in the United States, perhaps the most challenging, unusual, new philosophy has been forged by a novelist: Ayn Rand. Miss Rand's point of view is still comparatively unknown in America, but if it ever did take hold, it would revolutionize our lives. And Ayn, to begin with, I wonder if I can ask you to capsulize—I know this is difficult—can you capsulize your philosophy? What is "Randism"?

AYN RAND

First of all, I do not call it "Randism" and I don't like that name. I call it "Objectivism" . . .

MIKE WALLACE

All right.

AYN RAND

. . . meaning a philosophy based on objective reality. Now, let me explain it as briefly as I can. First, my philosophy is based on the concept that reality exists as an objective absolute. That man's mind—reason—is his means of perceiving it and that man needs a rational morality. I am primarily the creator of a new code of morality which has so far been believed impossible. Namely, a morality not based on faith . . .

MIKE WALLACE

On faith?

AYN RAND

Not on faith. Not on arbitrary whim, not on emotion, not on arbitrary edict—mystical or social—but on reason. A morality which can be proved by means of logic, which can be demonstrated to be true and necessary.

February 2, 1905. St. Petersburg, Russia. Alisa Rosenbaum came into a world wrought with revolution and oppression. It was a country on the brink of war—not a war between nations, but a war against the individual. A war that would make way for a form of collectivism history was never to forget.

Even at an early age, Ayn Rand did not believe in God or in destiny, but she did hold the conviction that there was a battle she must fight. A battle in the name of a truth that was as clear to her as the red flags and blood-stained streets of her native St. Petersburg. A battle to hold an individual spirit above the dark, murderous horde that was enveloping her country.

"I had to get out of Russia," she later wrote,
"if I wanted a chance ever to be alive."

A yn Rand did get out of Russia. She escaped to America and became one of the most controversial thinkers of the twentieth century. Her philosophy gained a worldwide audience and her ideas are now a part of university textbooks and curricula. Her novels, *The Fountainhead* and *Atlas Shrugged*, sell over 200,000 copies each year. And according to a joint survey by the Library of Congress and the Book-of-the-Month Club in 1991, *Atlas Shrugged* was named the second most influential book for Americans—following the Bible.

Ayn's father, Zinovy Zacharovich Rosenbaum.

Ayn, age nine, with her father in Switzerland.

Ayn's father was a self-made man who ran his own pharmacy. He created a middle-class lifestyle for his wife, Ayn and her two younger sisters, Natasha and Nora. Mr. Rosenbaum was conscientious about his work and was proud of his success. Ayn saw him as a principled man of unbending character.

Ayn's mother saw herself as an intellectual, attending lectures, French theater and holding salons in her home. Prone to fits of anger, Mrs. Rosenbaum would often comment to Ayn that raising children was a "hateful duty." Ayn, however, didn't take her mother literally, since her mother showed a great deal of concern for the family's health and welfare.

"Ayn Rand talked very little about Russia or her past in Russia. As I understand, she felt closer to her father than to her mother. She felt that she and her father had an intellectual understanding, whereas she and her mother were completely at odds. She always would preface any statement against her mother by her consciousness of how indebted she was to her mother, because her mother was the one who helped her leave Russia and insisted that Ayn would die if she had to stay in Russia."

Ayn (left) with her mother and her sister Natasha.

Left to right: Natasha, Nora and Ayn.

Natasha, two and a half years younger than Ayn—was very feminine and preoccupied with boys and clothes. Nora shared with Ayn a common interest in books, movies and movie actors. She wanted to be an artist and drew voraciously on any piece of paper she could find. Full of color and glamour, Nora's imaginative paintings expressed Ayn's sense of what the world outside the dreary Russian boundaries could be.

Nora with some of her drawings hanging on the wall behind her, circa 1934.

Nora's illustrations sent to Ayn in America.

Left to right: Nora, Ayn and Natasha.

But, unlike her sisters, more than anything, Ayn longed to be an adult entity. Not particularly outgoing in a social setting, she would become violently aroused when discussing ideas. She had no interest in approval or acceptance from her parents or others—consciously aware that anything she valued had to come from within herself. This remarkable independence was to be the benchmark of her own, distinctive outlook on life.

Ayn, front row with bow and arrow. Ayn's mother, back row middle.
Probably at a summer resort in Finland.

CANADIAN CAPERS

N. B. The bass notes indicated thus: ◆ may be omitted and the bass board struck with the foot.

GUS CHANDLER, BERT WHITE
and HENRY COHEN

In the summers of her youth, Ayn and her family traveled beyond the borders of Russia to resorts in Switzerland and Finland. Days were spent on the beach or in parks, where military bands often played. This was Ayn's introduction to what was to become her favorite music—what she later referred to as "tiddlywink" music.

LEONARD PEIKOFF

"Tiddlywink music was basically turn-of-the-century popular music of which there is no equivalent today. Completely joyful, but unserious, unheavy, light-hearted, fast rhythms—'Canadian Capers' might be an example—or there was an old song she liked called 'Get Out and Get Under' (to crank your model-T Ford), and that was her top favorite sense of life music."

It was the shimmering notes of the tiddlywink music that transported the young Ayn Rand to a world of light and air. A world she could now only imagine—a world abroad.

In two bounds the monstrous beast fell upon the engineer.

Noticing that Ayn didn't enjoy reading the dark Russian fairy tales or children's stories that her sisters liked, Ayn's mother subscribed to a French boys magazine.

The Mysterious Valley was a Rudyard Kipling-like serial. It was the story of English officers in India who were being attacked by huge, trained tigers and carried off into the jungle. An illustration of the hero, Cyrus Paltons—who does not appear until well into the story—mesmerized Ayn.

"She told me several times that that was the book she read at nine, *The Mysterious Valley*, and that Cyrus, the British hero of that story, was her first real concept of a hero. That she was in love with him, so far as you could be at the age of nine. And that all of her later heroes were developments from that. This is why when she got to *We the Living* and she did not yet feel ready to write about man the hero, she gave the character—the lead character, the woman—the name Kira, which is the female of Cyrus in Russian."

One scene in the story depicts the English prisoners being carried through the streets in a cage. They're all on the floor of the cage, cringing. Only Cyrus stands, gripping the bars. Self-confident and defiant, he swears at the evil Raja that he will get even no matter how much torture he must go through. "He is not afraid of anything and he has a purpose . . ." Ayn thought, ". . . intelligence, independence, courage—the heroic man. . . . This is what's important in life."

Courtesy Atlantean Press

He made hardly a sound.

Courtesy Atlantean Press

And there were men in the cage.

Cyrus was the projection of purposefulness and strength that now became the masculine qualities at the core of Ayn's romantic and literary desires.

CYRUS

HARRY BINSWANGER

"She thought of herself
as a woman, enjoyed
being a woman.
But she was the
opposite of a feminist.

Man worship was very
important to her and
her idea of femininity
was that it was a
woman's admiration
for masculine qualities."

ow that Ayn had discovered the kind of story and hero she could admire, she made the conscious decision to become a writer at the age of nine. Her mother took her to see her first movie, and Ayn quickly developed a passion for writing movie scenarios.

Then, one day, from her house on the big public square in St. Petersburg, she saw red flags rise up on the streets. Armed cossacks appeared and one man descended from a horse. He walked into the crowd, raised his sword and then brought it down. The year was 1917—a revolution had begun.

Called the "Bloodless Revolution," it was led by Alexander Kerensky against the czar. A great orator, Kerensky inspired an atmosphere of hope in the people of Russia. Amidst an unbridled exchange of ideas, he promised freedom from oppression and became the head of a provisional government. To the twelve-year-old Ayn, it seemed as if he was speaking out for her and for individualism. But in October of that same year, another revolution took place.

Ayn watched helplessly as the Bolsheviks marched in and closed her father's business. Placing a red seal over the door, the family was now officially expected to starve.

Victor Hugo
Courtesy Bettman Archives

Spurred on by the revolution, Ayn soon formed the conviction that communism—the idea that man should live for the state—was an abhorrent concept. She read newspapers and political pamphlets and made many anti-communist entries in her diary.

She continued to write stories, but her manner of thinking had changed. Since her interest in politics had intensified during the revolution, she wanted to create much more serious plots and important themes. Aspiring to the same caliber of writing as Dostoyevsky, she was inspired on an intensely personal level by the books her mother would read to her grandmother—the books of Victor Hugo.

"Hugo gives me the feeling of entering a cathedral," she once wrote. For Ayn, discovering such books as *The Man Who Laughs* and *Les Misérables*, was tantamount to stepping into Atlantis. Although she disagreed with Hugo's explicit philosophy, she became consciously aware that she wanted to write with the same literary grandeur and heroic scale. She thought, "This was how one should view life."

Not willing to accept any idea on faith, at the age of twelve, Ayn Rand seriously weighed the concept of God. If God represented the highest possible to man, she reasoned, then man—by nature—is inferior to God and can never reach that ideal. Considering this a degrading and unfounded claim, she simply made an entry in her diary: "Today I have decided to be an atheist."

The Orthodox Russian religion that permeated the country was never a serious concern for her. She knew that those around her were not representative of mankind. Someday she would find "her kind of people"—rational, purposeful, happy people. And that a proper life would begin "beyond the border."

LEONARD PEIKOFF

"Ayn Rand, in general, hated Russia—pre-communist and post-communist. She thought it was a mystical, backward, uncivilized country, that it was perfectly logical that the czarist regime should give rise to communism, and that the only thing to do is to get as far from it as she could."

The Phil Donahue Show (1980)

AYN RAND

It is the ugliest and, incidentally, the most mystical country on earth.

PHIL DONAHUE

But they're the ones that decry atheism, they're singing your song . . .

AYN RAND

Oh, no.

PHIL DONAHUE

I'm sorry, "decry Christianity." I'm sorry, "decry religion" is what I meant to say.

AYN RAND

They really don't. They have a materialistic mysticism of their own. Because if the mystics—the religionist people—tell you the mind . . . well, they don't speak of the mind . . . but, usually, the soul is the only thing of value about you, the body is evil and the Russians will say, "No, there isn't such a thing as a soul or mind, there's only your body." It's materialism. They believe that you're not a man but a collection of atoms.

PHIL DONAHUE

And give that body to the State for the collective effort of the . . .

AYN RAND

That's right. For the good of the whole and sacrifice to the State. And whoever says it, is or wants to be the State.

Artist rendition of map of Russia.
Art Credit: Maurice Hunt

In 1918, Mr. Rosenbaum moved his family out of St. Petersburg to escape the Communists. Thinking the Bolsheviks would not remain in power for long, he was optimistic that the family would return to reclaim his business and his property. Almost killed by bandits near Odessa, they finally made it to the Crimean Peninsula, where he opened an apothecary. The country was riddled with black markets and food shortages. It wasn't long before his new business was nationalized. In 1921, Ayn graduated from high school, while the Red Army now also occupied the Crimea. Mr. Rosenbaum, still hoping to regain his rightful belongings, decided to move the family back to St. Petersburg, which was now called Petrograd.

It was on this trip that the sixteen-year-old Ayn caught her first sight of Moscow. She was suddenly struck by the thought of how many people there were in the world. She felt a door opening and the nature of her ambition took shape—to communicate through her writing that life had a profound and special meaning.

What can we know about the universe?

The Phil Donahue Show (1980)

AYN RAND

Every argument for the existence of God is incomplete and improper and has been refuted, and people go on and on because they want to believe. Well, I regard it as evil to place your emotions—your desire—above the evidence of what your mind knows.

PHIL DONAHUE

And I regard it as intellectually lazy to look at the universe and to suggest, as you seem to be doing, that this is some accident.

AYN RAND

I didn't say that.

PHIL DONAHUE

Well, how in the world did we get all this order? Aren't you impressed with that?

AYN RAND

No. Order is only in good cases in the minds of our scientists who are able to understand some part of it. But there isn't an artificial order in the universe and it's not chance. What would be the alternative? Nature. That the universe (and remember, the universe is everything that exists) has always been here. Because you cannot discuss or know anything about what was here before anything existed. That's what you're doing with the idea of God— speaking philosophically.

PHIL DONAHUE

True.

AYN RAND

You say you need someone to explain the order but what will you have then to explain God?

41

At sixteen, Ayn entered the University of Leningrad as a history major. Although teacher after teacher bored her, it was the discovery of great philosophers such as Aristotle and St. Thomas Aquinas that intensely aroused her.

For Ayn, Aristotle's belief "that there is only one reality, the one that man perceives . . . and that his mind is his only tool of knowledge,"* became the core of her own philosophic thought. It also conflicted with the dominant philosophic view, originated by Plato, that there is a supernatural realm beyond the world we see.

HARRY BINSWANGER

"When she was a college student at the University of Leningrad at age nineteen or twenty, she took a course in ancient philosophy from Professor Lossky, who was a distinguished expert in the field of ancient philosophy. When it came time for her to take her final exam, he asked her questions almost exclusively about Plato and none about Aristotle. Of course, she despised Plato, even then . . ."

LEONARD PEIKOFF

"And he said to her, 'You don't seem to agree with Plato,' implying, '. . . well, what are your views?' And her answer was, 'My views are not yet part of the history of philosophy, but they will be.'"

Ayn (lower left) with her high school graduating class, Yevpatoria, Crimea, 1921.

HARRY BINSWANGER

"So, that was another example. Both of her objectivity—that she didn't want to argue with a Platonist about the merits of Plato and Aristotle, being just a student—her independence—that it didn't bother her that he disagreed and she wasn't out to sell him on her views—and of her ability to counter the male prejudice that existed in that Victorian society against women intellectuals."

Under the Communist regime, life had degenerated into a new level of hell. Hunger had engulfed the nation, and there were deadly epidemics of typhus—the "disease of dirt." Very outspoken at first, Ayn was reckless in making anti-Soviet remarks at the university. She witnessed many purges that resulted in students and their families being sent to Siberia at a moment's notice. Realizing she was placing her entire family in danger, she became more cautious while expressing her point of view.

But amidst the drudgery, Ayn found something to look forward to. She discovered the world of operettas. She walked to school instead of taking the tram so she could afford to buy tickets. She waited four hours in the cold to be first in line to see *The Gypsy Princess* by Kálmán, Lehar's *Where the Lark Sings* or Millöcker's *The Beggar Student*. Here she saw a world of top hats and ballrooms. Sometimes the stage would display lighted streets of a foreign city, and she would later think, "It was the world into which I had to grow up someday, the world I had to reach."

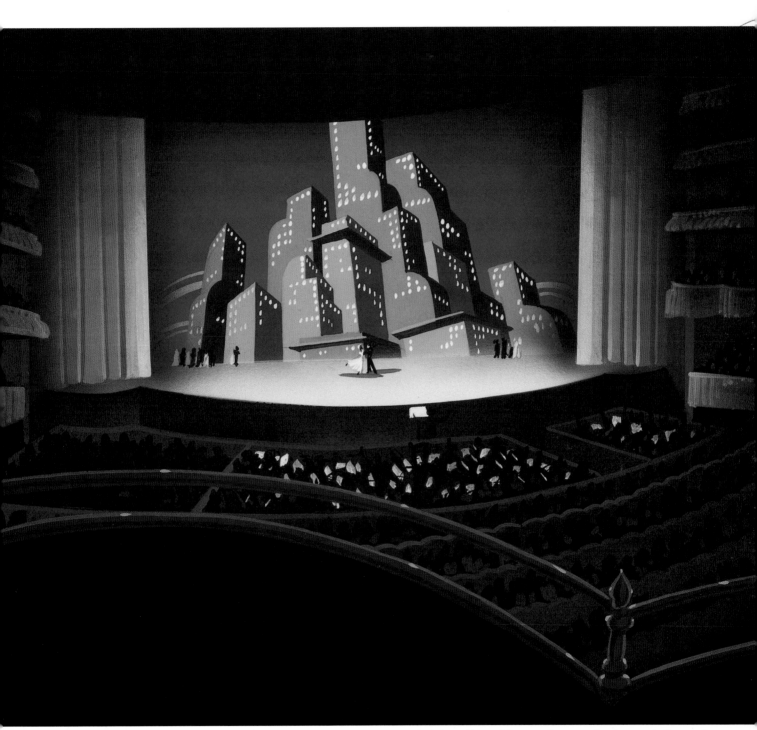

Artist's rendition of the type of operetta that Ayn saw in Petrograd.
Art Credit: Jim Hickey

But it was the flicker of projectors and the images on movie screens that truly enraptured her. She and her sister Nora loved the glamorous, plot-driven films of Cecil B. DeMille. And the expressionistic *Siegfried*—by her favorite German director, Fritz Lang—became a glowing source of inspiration to her.

Siegfried, *1923*
courtesy of The Academy of
Motion Picture Arts and Sciences

Movies like *The Mark of Zorro*, *The Oyster Princess*, *The Indian Tomb* and *The Isle of Lost Ships* had a "sense of adventure"* with self-reliant heroes accomplishing great feats.

The Mark of Zorro, *1920.*
Courtesy Worldview Entertainment, Inc. and
The Academy of Motion Picture Arts and Sciences

After graduating from college, in the fall of
1924, she entered a school for screenwriters
called the Cinema Institute. The first year at
the institute was focused on acting, and
Ayn diligently studied the art of performing
for the silent screen.

With an insatiable appetite for anything "abroad," Ayn would sit through two shows of a movie just to catch a glimpse of the New York skyline in a scene. Like "a shot in the arm"* and "a life-saving transfusion,"* it was wiping Russia as a world out of her consciousness and inciting her to write stories of her own. Stories completely untouched by the misery of the life she was desperate to escape.

LEONARD PEIKOFF

"The Russian sense of life was mystical, hopeless, authoritarian, obedient, malevolent. And the American sense of life was optimistic, 'can-do,' achievement-oriented, benevolent. They were exact opposites. The Americans wanted the world to make sense. They believed in common sense. The Russians were deep in this incredible mysticism of either the communist dialectic process or Holy Mother Russia from the religious side. So, the two countries were diametric opposites. And she had the misfortune or fortune to be born a thorough American in her soul in the heart of this Russian religion turning into communism. So, it was antipathy from day one."

We the Living (1942)

VICTOR

How old are you?

KIRA

Eighteen.

VICTOR

Eighteen. Good age to set your goals in life. Get yourself a job in a Soviet office. That's the most promising career for a woman.

KIRA

That kind of career doesn't interest me.

UNCLE VASILI

Kira, you needn't take such talk seriously.

VICTOR

One must be practical these days. Kira, typewriter keys are the stepping stones to higher office.

UNCLE VASILI

Enough of this talk!

IRENA

Kira, aren't you interested in this?

KIRA

I am. But it's superfluous. I'm going to be an engineer.

VICTOR

Then come to the Technological Institute with me . . . and build for the Red State.

KIRA

I'll build because I want to build. It's the only profession where I don't have to lie. Numbers are numbers. Steel is steel.

VICTOR

An engineer. You think that's suitable for a woman?

UNCLE VASILI

Child, what are you doing in the Soviet Union?

KIRA

That's what I'm wondering about.

Alida Valli as Kira in the 1942 filmed version of We the Living.
Courtesy of Duncan Scott Productions

$\mathcal{W}$hile still attending the Cinema Institute in 1925, Ayn also worked at a meaningless job as a museum guide. But she went through her days with only one thought: to go abroad. Sympathetic to Ayn's goal, Mrs. Rosenbaum wrote to relatives in Chicago and asked if Ayn could visit them in America.

Ayn as a guide at the Peter and Paul Fortress Museum.

In the fall of 1925, Ayn received a foreign passport that was valid for six months. In order to secure a first-class cabin on a boat to America, Mrs. Rosenbaum sold her jewelry. At a small going-away party, Ayn could sense her impending freedom.

But it was an acquaintance, speaking in a hushed, hopeless voice, that moved her. He said, "If they ask you, in America, tell them that Russia is a huge cemetery and that we are all slowly dying."

A short time later, Ayn watched that cemetery recede past her train window. She had promised to tell them in America.

Crowd scene courtesy Archive Films

But now, like a heart skipping beats in anticipation, she made her way across Europe. Stopping in Berlin, she visited a relative and celebrated her twenty-first birthday. Finally, from the deck of her ship as it set to sea from Le Havre, it struck her that she would not be back. This was what she would later call an "overture,"* "the turning point"* she'd been waiting for.

Ayn and her cousin Vera Guzarchik

*I*n February 1926, Ayn's boat arrived in New York harbor where a heavy fog had settled in. Immigrants were asked to wait in a salon on the ship while officials checked their papers. When Ayn finally reached the deck, she was crushed to find out that the boat had already docked. She had missed the Statue of Liberty and the New York skyline. But then, as she descended from the boat, a light snow began to fall. She later described the experience: "It was dark by then, it was kind of early evening, I think about seven o'clock or so. And seeing the first lighted skyscrapers—it was snowing, very faintly, and I think I began to cry because I remember feeling the snowflakes and the tears sort of together. . . ."

Opposite: New York Harbor.
Courtesy Film Bank

Staying with relatives, she spent a few days in New York and saw Broadway at night for the first time. Stunned by the neon signs, she also saw her first movie in America. She then went on to Chicago, anxious to start her career as a screenwriter and get out on her own. Not yet able to write very well in English, she thought she could at least write for silent films, which did not rely on dialogue.

Lillian and Dorothy Gish, Orphans of the Storm, *1922.*
Courtesy Worldview Entertainment, Inc.

One of her relatives in Chicago owned a movie theater, and Ayn went to the movies daily. This helped her master the English language enough to write four movie originals over a period of six months. One was called "The Skyscraper," which was a wild, exaggerated story about a "noble" crook who jumps from skyscraper to skyscraper with the aid of a parachute.

Aware of Ayn's passion for becoming a screenwriter, her relatives in Chicago were able—through a movie distributor they knew—to secure a letter of recommendation to the DeMille Studios. Borrowing one hundred dollars, Ayn set off by train for Hollywood in August of 1926. Upon her arrival, she found residence at the Hollywood Studio Club, a home created especially for young women seeking a start in the movie business. It housed other hopefuls who later became Ginger Rogers, Marilyn Monroe and Kim Novak.

Wanting to adopt a new professional name, she chose "Ayn." Using a Finnish feminine name, pronounced "I-na," she dropped the final "a" and got "Ine." Keeping the "R" from Rosenbaum, she chose "Rand" for her surname. She also hoped that her new name would protect her family from the anti-Soviet remarks she was bound to make in America.

The next day, with letter of recommendation in hand, she set out for the DeMille Studios. Arriving at the gate, she went to the publicity department, where she was interviewed for a junior screenwriting position. After being told there were no jobs, she walked back to the gate. Suddenly, she was stunned to see DeMille himself sitting in an open roadster. As he drove past the girl with the large eyes staring at him, he stopped and asked where she was from.

When she explained that she had just arrived from Russia and that he was her favorite director, he invited her to accompany him. Despite her shock at riding with DeMille, she told him that she wanted to be a screenwriter. Driving through the back lot of the studio, they arrived at the set of DeMille's current picture, *The King of Kings*.

Sincerely yours —

Cecil B. de Mille

DeMille on the set of The King of Kings, *1926.*
Courtesy Richard Gordon Films, Inc. and
The Academy of Motion Picture Arts and Sciences.

DeMille explained that if Ayn wanted to work in pictures, she should learn by watching. She spent the day observing the film company at work. She breathlessly watched as they set up shots and DeMille directed the actors. She was invited to join the cast and crew for lunch but politely declined, despite her hunger pains. At the end of the day, DeMille located her and gave her a personally signed pass to return to the set the next day.

For several days, DeMille continued to give Ayn personal passes to the set. He would approach her between shots and explain the process of filmmaking. He found Ayn's background "exotic" and nick-named her "Caviar." When he discovered her precarious financial situation, he immediately offered her a job as an extra.

DeMille with his cast for The King of Kings, *1925.*
Courtesy Richard Gordon Films, Inc. and
The Academy of Motion Picture Arts and Sciences.

DeMille Directing Extras

DeMILLE
All right, now, you people—you townspeople over beyond the gates there—come on, work yourselves into . . . into the emotions of such a scene. Don't be extras! Be a nation!

Ayn Rand in The King of Kings.
Courtesy Richard Gordon Films, Inc. and
The Academy of Motion Picture Arts and Sciences.

Ayn Rand in The King of Kings.
*Courtesy Richard Gordon Films, Inc. and
The Academy of Motion Picture Arts and Sciences.*

Ayn Rand in The King of Kings.
*Courtesy Richard Gordon Films, Inc. and
The Academy of Motion Picture Arts and Sciences.*

Ayn on the roof of her Gower Street apartment in Hollywood.

She finally wrote to her family and informed them of her new name and that she was officially in the movies.

MICHAEL S. BERLINER

"I would say that Ayn Rand's life was a focal point for their concern as a family in Russia. They would receive a letter from her and the whole family would come over—the aunts, the uncles, the cousins— and there would be a reading of a letter from her. Her sister Nora, with whom Ayn Rand shared a tremendous interest in the movies, would draw little pictures at the bottom of the letters showing 'Ayn Rand' in lights. So, Ayn Rand getting into the movies was a goal and the most exciting thing that ever happened. When she finally told them of her meeting with Cecil B. DeMille in 1926, it must have been like an earthquake to her family. And her father, who was not very expressive, wrote that he could not sleep all night."

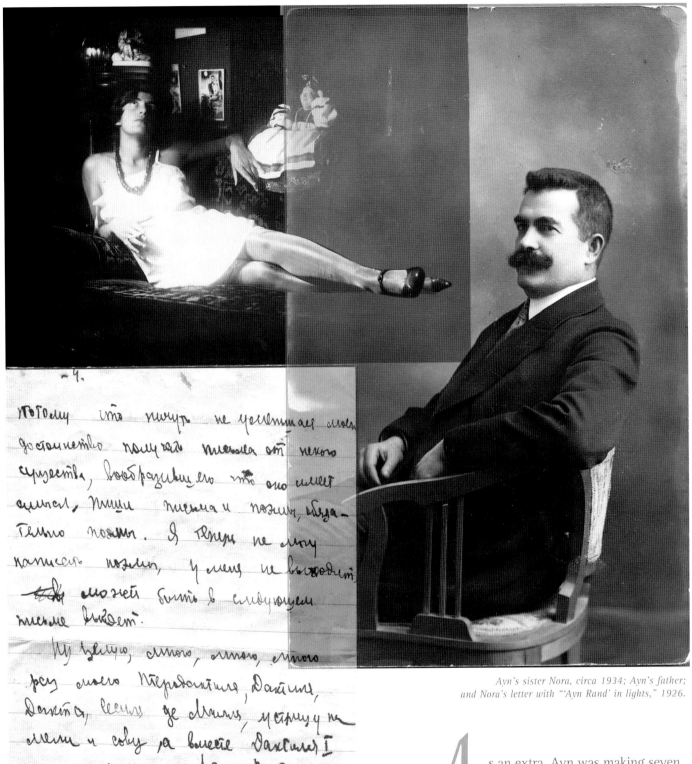

*Ayn's sister Nora, circa 1934; Ayn's father;
and Nora's letter with "Ayn Rand' in lights," 1926.*

As an extra, Ayn was making seven dollars and fifty cents a day. For several months, De Mille would call her in to work whenever possible. She slowly warmed up to the cast, which included H. B. Warner as Christ and Joseph Schildkraut as Judas. Schildkraut even took her out to lunch, flirted with her and then gave her an autographed picture.

MY IDEAL FACE

Two days after securing a job with DeMille, she was riding the streetcar to the studio and spotted a tall, handsome man across the aisle from her.

She thought, "this [is] my ideal face." It was a face she later sketched from memory— a memory that was actually "love at first sight." To her surprise, not only did this man get off the streetcar at the same stop, he entered the DeMille Studio gate as well. Later that day, she spotted him on the set of *The King of Kings* and discovered he was an actor in a bit part.

Frank O'Connor (second soldier from the left, with shield) in a scene from The King of Kings.
Courtesy Richard Gordon Films, Inc. and
The Academy of Motion Picture Arts and Sciences.

Frank O'Connor was born in Lorraine, Ohio, in 1897, one of seven children. After his mother's early death, he worked his way to New York hoping to make it in the movies. Helping a driver change a flat tire on a Griffith Studios truck, Frank asked to be taken to the studio as payment. A great fan of D. W. Griffith, soon he had his first movie job in *Orphans of the Storm* starring Lillian and Dorothy Gish.

Frank (second from left) with his brothers and sisters, 1907.

Griffith's success with *Orphans of the Storm* was to be his last, and the studio eventually moved to California. At the age of twenty-eight, Frank worked as a steward on a freighter through the Panama Canal to join his brothers Joe and Nick in Hollywood. The first job he got when he arrived was on *The King of Kings*.

Now, quietly milling about the set, waiting for the next set-up, Frank kept to himself. At a distance, Ayn "followed him like a camera"* and desperately tried to think of a way to meet him.

A few days later, during a scene where Christ carries the cross through the city of Jerusalem, Ayn watched carefully as Frank hit his marks on the first take. On the second take, she maneuvered herself to get in his way. He stepped on her foot and apologized. From that moment on, they didn't stop talking. Frank later commented to his brother Nick, "Today I met a very interesting and funny Russian on the set—I couldn't understand a word she said."

Since it was Frank's last day of work on the film and they hadn't exchanged numbers, Ayn feared she would never see him again. Although the casting office would not give out Frank's number, she did not give up hope. She felt a "benevolent inevitability"* that they would meet again.

AYN & FRANK'S THEME
Britting
1995
Andantino teneramente
mp dolce e ben legato
cresc.
mf
mp
espr.
cresc.

The Skyscraper

The Story of a Man

Ayn's notes from The Skyscraper *project.*

Eventually, Ayn gave her four scenarios to DeMille to read. However, the woman in charge of his scenario department disliked Ayn on sight and gave the stories a very bad report, calling them "improbable, far-fetched," and "not human enough."

Despite this report, DeMille hired Ayn as a junior screenwriter at twenty-five dollars a week. This meant that she would do treatments and synopsize already purchased properties. Because DeMille considered a construction site an interesting backdrop for a film, a novel called *The Skyscraper* was the first project Ayn was assigned to.

The Broadway department store at the corner of Hollywood and Vine.
Courtesy Security Pacific Collection

Required to do research, Ayn made an appointment to visit the construction site of The Broadway department store at the corner of Hollywood and Vine. Informed that her appointment was delayed, she walked around the corner to the library on Ivar Street to wait. She entered the building and, amidst the hush of turning pages, she saw Frank O'Connor reading a book. It turned out that he, too, was waiting for an appointment.

He looked up at her and smiled in recognition.

They went outside to talk and their courtship officially began. Ayn was twenty-two and Frank was twenty-nine.

*W*ith the depression approaching, DeMille closed his studio in 1928, and Ayn could only find odd jobs. She was now surviving on thirty cents a day and living on very little food. Although she had previously been sending her family money, they were now sending some to her.

She continued to write with fierce persistence and made notes to discipline herself. "From now on," she wrote, "no thought whatever about yourself, only about your work. You don't exist. You are only a writing engine. Don't stop, until you really and honestly know that you cannot go on. . . . Stop admiring yourself—you are nothing yet."

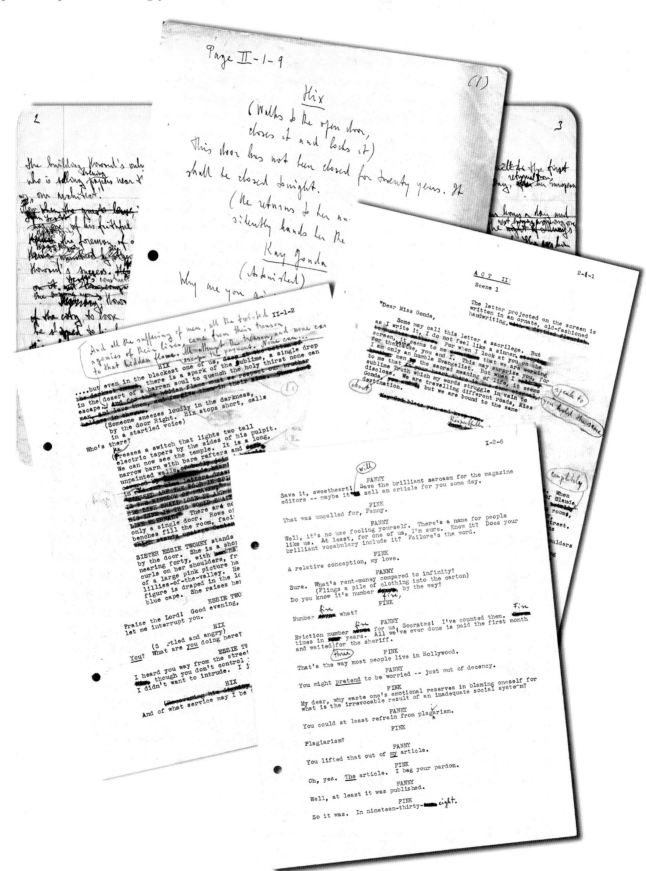

uring this period, Ayn didn't want Frank to know she was struggling or think she needed help. But he was struggling as well, because acting jobs had become scarce. Dating for them consisted of going for walks, visits to the beach and an occasional movie. After several extensions, Ayn only had one month left before her visa was to expire. Although Frank's brother Nick joked that he would marry her to keep her in America, there was no need to discuss the matter.

On April 15, 1929—the same month her visa was to expire—Ayn and Frank were married by a judge. They then drove through the desert to Mexicali and spent a sleepless night in the heat. The next day Ayn drove back into the country as the wife of an American.

What is romantic love?

Day at Night (1974)

INTERVIEWER
How does the concept of love fit into this philosophy?

AYN RAND
You fall in love with a person because you regard him or her as a value and because they contribute to your personal happiness. Now, you couldn't fall in love with a person by saying, "You mean nothing to me. I don't care whether you live or die, but you need me and, therefore, I'm in love with you." If someone offered love of that kind, everyone would regard that as a deadly insult. That isn't love. Therefore, romantic love is a selfish emotion. It is the choice of a person as a great value, and what you fall in love with is the same values—which you choose—embodied in another person.

LEONARD PEIKOFF

"She regarded love as an extremely selfish emotion. It was a response to your greatest values in the person and character of another person. So you had to know them well and they had to, in all essentials, be exactly what you wanted from another human being. If so, it was one of the greatest of all values. But it was not *the* top value. She regarded career as the top value, because she felt that if you tried to base a life exclusively on your relation to another person—however wonderful or however much in love—it's going to end up being a relationship of dependence. Each person has to have their own creative goal, and they must be like two individuals traveling on the same journey but happen to find that they are going on the same journey together. And then love is a fantastic supplement to their individual creativity."

Ayn and Frank with friend, actress Mary Carr.

With Frank O'Connor by her side, Ayn continued her struggle to write and make ends meet in Hollywood. In 1929, she took a job as a filing clerk at the RKO wardrobe department for twenty dollars a week. Although she hated the job, it was a financial oasis in the depression. In six months, she earned a raise and within a year became head of the department. Soon Ayn and Frank were able to buy their first car. Since Frank was also working, he presented Ayn with a made-to-order desk, a radio and her first portable typewriter.

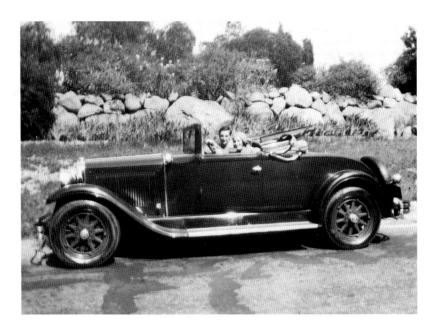

Despite her long hours in the wardrobe department, she wrote in every spare moment she could find. Even though she officially made notes for her first novel, writing for the movies was still an important goal for her.

MICHAEL S. BERLINER

"She was a tremendous movie fan in her early years and kept a diary, which we found, of seemingly every movie she attended from 1922 until early 1929. There were 433 entries and she kept a detailed record of every one, underlining actors she liked the best and grading the movie. The actors and actresses that she liked she would give one underline, that she liked a lot, she would give two underlines, that she really loved, she would give three underlines.

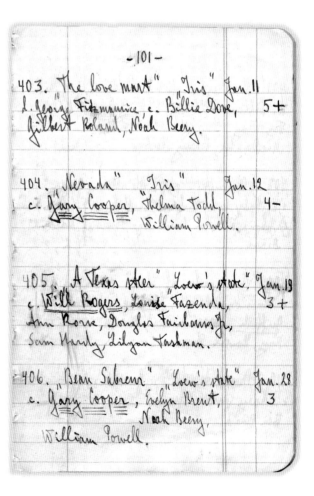

Movie Diary pages from 1926. Note Ayn's reference to herself and Frank as extras in The King of Kings *entry "(A.R. - F.O'C)."*

"In the back of the movie diary, I found a little piece of paper in which she had listed her favorite actors and actresses. Many of these actors and actresses that she loved in the 1920s, when she was in Russia, and were really her window into civilization—which is the West—she later met."

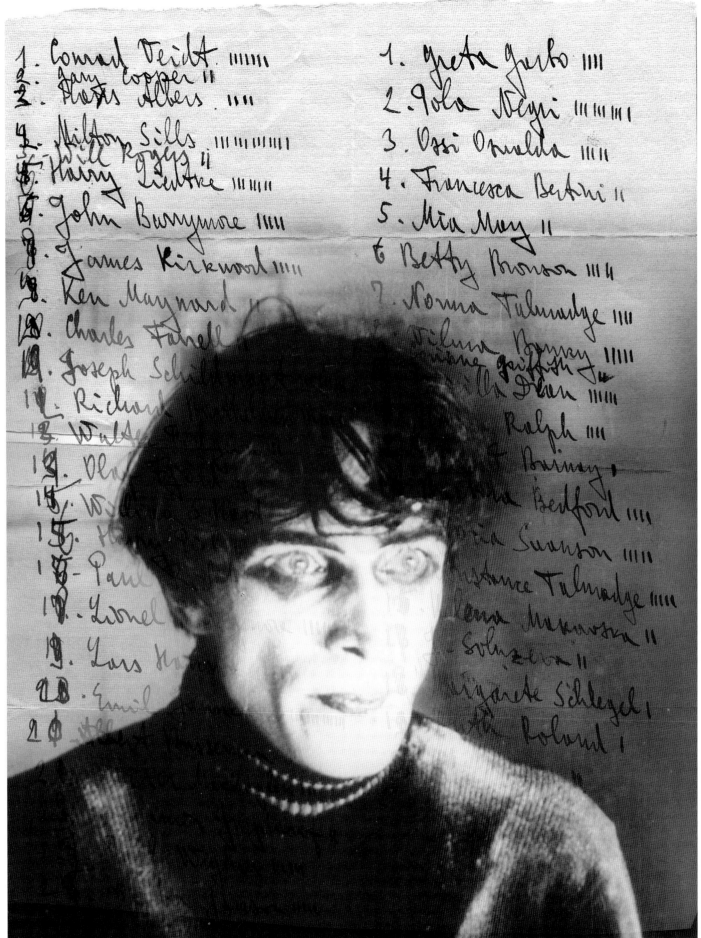

1. Conrad Veidt. ||||||
2. Gary Cooper ||
3. Hans Albers . ||||
4. Milton Sills ||||||||||
5. Will Rogers ||
6. Harry Liedtke ||||||
7. John Barrymore ||||
8. James Kirkwood ||||
9. Ken Maynard
10. Charles Farrell
11. Joseph Schildkraut
12. Richard
13. Walter
14. Ole
15. Ws
16. Ha
17. Paul
18. Lionel
19. Lars
20. Emil
21.

1. Greta Garbo ||||
2. Pola Negri |||| ||||
3. Ossi Oswalda ||||
4. Francesca Bertini ||
5. Mia May ||
6. Betty Bronson ||||||
7. Norma Talmadge ||||
   Wilma Banky ||||||
   Corinne Griffith
   Priscilla Dean ||||||
   Ralph ||||
   Rosimay |
   Bedford ||||
   Swanson ||||||
   Constance Talmadge ||||
   Lena Makowska ||
   Solnzeva ||
   Margarete Schlegel |
   Roland |

Ayn's favorite actor, Conrad Veidt, in one of his many exotic roles.

Left to right: Conrad Veidt (in The Indian Tomb),
Mia May and Ethel Barrymore.

To Miss Jyn Rand. With admiration and gratitude and love Gloria Swanson 1940

MICHAEL S. BERLINER

"One of the interesting things in this list that she kept of her favorite movie actors and actresses is to find Gary Cooper up in number two—originally he hadn't been on the list at all. She saw him in movies, I think, in 1928 and pushed him up into number two, right before Conrad Veidt. Then, she changed the numbers on everyone below Gary Cooper. And, then, of course, almost twenty years later, there's Gary Cooper playing Howard Roark in her own movie."

Gary Cooper with Ayn. Publicity still for The Fountainhead *movie, 1949.*
Courtesy Warner Bros.

Continuing her struggle to master English, she wrote a variety of short stories and plays. One such play, called *Ideal*, embraced her passion for the movies and admiration for her favorite actress, Greta Garbo.

Janne Peters as Kay Gonda in Ideal.
Photo: James Sorenson

The story, set in Hollywood, 1934, follows a fictitious movie star—named Kay Gonda—on her quest to find one man of integrity among her fans. In this scene, we get a glimpse at an early formulation of Ayn Rand's ideal man.

"Ideal" Dramatization

KAY GONDA

I saw a man once, when I was very young. He stood on a rock, high in the mountains. His arms were spread out and his body bent backward, and I could see him as an arc against the sky. He stood still and tense, like a string trembling to a note of ecstasy no man had ever heard. I have never known who he was. I knew only that this was what life should be.

ESTERHAZY

And?

KAY GONDA
(in a changed voice)

And I came home, and my mother was serving supper, and she was happy because the roast had a thick gravy. And she gave a prayer of thanks to God for it . . .

(whirls to him suddenly, angrily)

Don't listen to me! Don't look at me like that! I've tried to renounce it. I thought I must close my eyes and bear anything and learn to live like the others. To make me as they were. To make me forget. But I can't forget the man on the rock. I can't!

While still working at RKO, Ayn wrote two scenarios about Russia in her spare time: "Red Pawn" and "Treason." In 1932, "Red Pawn," a story about the evil of dictatorship, was bought by Universal for the sum of fifteen hundred dollars. Eventually, "Red Pawn" was traded to Paramount as a vehicle for Marlene Dietrich. But not wanting to do another story set in Russia, Dietrich's director, Josef von Sternberg, decided against the project and the film was never made.

Ayn in 1936.

MICHAEL S. BERLINER

"It was her first sale and it really established herself as a professional writer. Now, some years later, she sent a copy of 'Red Pawn' to Cecil B. DeMille and she said:

'I have always hoped that I would not drop out of sight entirely. That the day would come when I would be successful enough to show you that you had not wasted the attention you had given me at my start in Hollywood. . . . I cannot say that I have accomplished a great deal yet. But, at least, I am a writer and I feel that I can now thank you from the bottom of my heart. . . .

Sincerely,
Ayn Rand'

And then she put in parentheses,
    'Caviar, if you remember.'"

Left to right: Mary Carr, unidentified friend and Ayn, early 1930s.

Ayn in Hollywood, early 1930s.

The sale of "Red Pawn" enabled Ayn to quit her job at RKO and write full time. She was finally free to finish her first novel, *We the Living.*

While working on the novel, she happened to see a play called *The Trial of Mary Dugan*, which took place in a courtroom. She had also read newspaper articles on the Swedish "Match King," Ivar Krueger—who had committed suicide and whose financial empire had fallen. She was interested in the fact that he was being denounced not for his dishonesty and fraud, but for the fact that he had been successful. She devised a play that centered on the trial of a woman accused of murdering an infamous industrialist. Titled *Penthouse Legend*, she created an unprecedented dramatic device which required members of the audience to be selected before each performance to serve on the jury. She conceived the play with two endings—one for a verdict of "not guilty" and one for "guilty."

LEONARD PEIKOFF

"She thought that the jury gimmick would be best if she had done it in conjunction with some hotly controversial issue like abortion, or trial marriages, or whatever. But she couldn't write about an issue of that narrow a scope, so she had to combine it with a 'sense of life' concern. And therefore, it's the jury making their final decision on balanced evidence according to their sense of life."

Night of January 16th *(1935)*
(formerly titled Penthouse Legend *and* Woman on Trial*).*
Courtesy New York Public Library for the Performing Arts. Lincoln Center

"*I*f this play's sense of life were to be verbalized," she later wrote, "it would say, in effect: 'Your life, your achievement, your happiness, your person are of paramount importance. Live up to your highest vision of yourself no matter what the circumstances you might encounter. An exalted view of self-esteem is man's most admirable quality.'"

Rejected by many producers who feared the gimmick would destroy the theatrical illusion, E. E. Clive—a character actor who ran the Hollywood Playhouse—finally produced *Penthouse Legend*. Opening as *Woman on Trial* in the spring of 1934, it starred Barbara Bedford, a silent-film actress, as Karen Andre. Although Clive was a good director and the play got rave reviews, hearing her words uttered by actors who didn't understand their meaning was a profound disappointment to Ayn. It was only the spectacle of her name on the marquee for the first time that thrilled her. Her sister Nora's image of success in America had now become a reality for Ayn.

After the run in Hollywood, producer Al Woods optioned the play for Broadway under the title *Night of January 16th*.

The cast of Woman on Trial *(1934). Ayn is third from left, middle row. Frank is behind her left shoulder. E. E. Clive is far right and Barbara Bedford (Karen Andre) to his right.*

The Hollywood Playhouse, 1934.

Meanwhile, Frank had been acting steadily, appearing in the films *Cimarron* and *Three on a Match*. But it was a variety of comedic roles that were to kill his ambition to work as an actor. Romantic roles that suited him were not to be found. He began to consider another career, while Ayn continued to write.

A year later, *Night of January 16th* went into rehearsals, and Ayn was thrust into a tortuous process of constantly protecting her script from changes.

When the play opened on Broadway in September 1935, she was emotionally spent. Not able to watch what the play had become, she sat in the back row and yawned.

Despite the mixed reviews, it was a moderately successful show that paid her royalties of up to twelve hundred dollars a week. The show ran for seven months, and night after night celebrities such as Jack Dempsey and Helen Keller sat in the jury box.

Doris Nolan and Walter Pidgeon in Night of January 16th.
Courtesy New York Public Library
for the Performing Arts, Lincoln Center

The stars, Doris Nolan and Walter Pidgeon, fared well as the lead characters. Ayn had suggested Pidgeon for the role of gangster, "Guts" Regan, and it ultimately led to an MGM movie contract for him.

But, in spite of the play's eventual popularity, Ayn was never to forget watching the integrity of her script destroyed.

However, she was now ready to focus entirely on the work she had complete control over—the final chapters of *We the Living.*

"*We the Living* is not a novel 'about Soviet Russia.' It is a novel about Man against the State," Ayn wrote. "Its basic theme is the sanctity of human life. . . . It is a story about dictatorship, any dictatorship, anywhere, at any time, whether it be Soviet Russia, Nazi Germany, or . . . a socialist America. . . ."

The heroine of the story, Kira Argounova, wants to be an engineer. An aluminum suspension bridge is the shimmering spectacle of achievement she aspires to. An individualist caught in the same revolutionary Russia that Ayn Rand had survived, Kira asks, "Don't you know that there are things, in the best of us, which no outside hand should dare to touch? Things sacred because, and only because, one can say, 'This is mine'? . . . Don't you know that there is something in us which must not be touched by any state, any collective, by any number of millions?"

In a foreword to the novel in 1958, Ayn wrote that "*We the Living* is as near to an autobiography as I will ever write. It is not an autobiography in the literal, but only in the intellectual, sense. The plot is invented; the background is not." Although Ayn was pleased with her characterizations in *We the Living*, she felt she hadn't yet fully achieved her style in the English language. She knew that was to come with practice. But when the manuscript was submitted by her agent, Ann Watkins, it was the fact that the story depicted the reality of Soviet Russia—a reality American intellectuals refused to believe—that resulted in it being rejected by one publisher after another.

Animation drawings by Cynthia Wells from A Sense of Life.

By 1936, with the New Deal in full swing, *We the Living* was finally sold to Macmillan. Macmillan's editors had been divided on whether to buy the book due to its anti-Soviet theme. When it was published, the company was not totally behind it, placing only two ads. Reviews claimed the author simply didn't understand the "great Soviet experiment."

Despite this, the novel was slowly building an audience.

"I wrote the book feeling that I was in some measure, in the only manner possible to me, repaying my adopted country for the freedom and the opportunity it has given me," Ayn wrote at the time. "How much good the book will accomplish I cannot say, and it is not up to me. . . . But if it can make a few people pause and doubt the glories of Communism, I shall feel satisfied."

At this time, producer Jerome Mayer approached Ayn to adapt *We the Living* for the stage.

LEONARD PEIKOFF

"She did not think *We the Living* was suitable to be performed as a play on Broadway. There was a tremendous amount of opposition from Hollywood stars, who would profess to her—Bette Davis is one example—that they would be honored to do the part, they would love to do Kira and, suddenly, two weeks or two months later, they would say, 'I'm sorry. My agent tells me that it will destroy my career.' Because it was Hollywood in the thirties. It was the 'Red Decade,' and to appear on the stage in an anti-Communist play—in that stage—meant it could be boycotted entirely by the leftists who owned Hollywood."

Animation drawings by Cynthia Wells from A Sense of Life.

Renamed *The Unconquered*, the renowned producer/director George Abbott eventually took on the project and the play went into production.

Abbott was mainly a comedy director and tried to mold the characters into the "folks next door." He constantly asked Ayn to change her austerely romantic dialogue to naturalistic approximations. Arguing with Abbot thoroughly disgusted her, and by the time the play opened, she had lost all interest in the production. The reviews were uniformly bad, and the play lasted only five performances.

Helen Craig as Kira and Dean Jagger as Andrei in The Unconquered *on Broadway, 1939.*
Courtesy New York Public Library for the Performing Arts, Lincoln Center

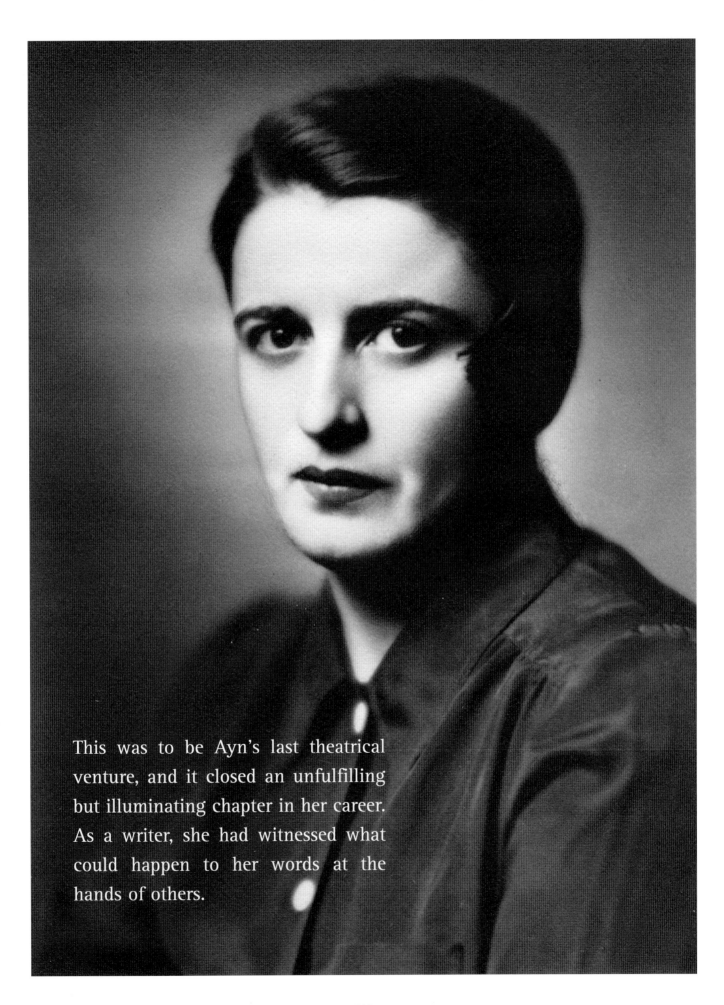

This was to be Ayn's last theatrical venture, and it closed an unfulfilling but illuminating chapter in her career. As a writer, she had witnessed what could happen to her words at the hands of others.

A few years later, Ayn met the Italian actress Alida Valli in Hollywood. Valli told Ayn that she had been instrumental in getting the film version of *We the Living* made in Italy in 1942. Without Ayn's knowledge, the film had been released and was very successful. But it wasn't long before Mussolini's government realized the story was an indictment of not only communism, but fascism as well. The film was pulled and placed in a vault. It was finally uncovered in the 1960s and restored with Ayn's approval.

In the Hollywood of the 1940s, Valli tried to persuade David O. Selznick to remake *We the Living*. But the "Red Decade" had a stronghold on American culture, and Ayn's plea to alert the world about the horrors of communism went unheard. She had underestimated the influence of altruism on American intellectuals.

Alida Valli as Kira in We the Living, *1942.*
Courtesy Duncan Scott Productions

The Phil Donahue Show (1980)

PHIL DONAHUE

You don't like altruists . . .

AYN RAND

I disapprove of them. I regard them as evil.

PHIL DONAHUE

Okay, but what . . . so, what's bad about the person who wants to help other people?

AYN RAND

Well, to begin with, that's the big mistake. People can want to help other people—properly and with very good reasons—but that isn't altruism. Altruism doesn't mean merely helping people. It means sacrificing yourself to others—placing the interests of others above your own. It's the self-sacrificing person who is an altruist.

PHIL DONAHUE

And what's wrong with that?

AYN RAND

What's wrong with suicide? What's wrong with giving up life, and why is the happiness of another person important and good but not your own?

PHIL DONAHUE

To sacrifice for your loved one is—in many cases—then, a misnomer.

AYN RAND

If you love your husband or wife and you have to, let us say, select between spending money for your spouse if he's ill or going to a nightclub. It's not a sacrifice to spend money for your spouse if he or she is your value. That is what you want to do . . .

PHIL DONAHUE

I see . . .

AYN RAND

But if you let, for instance, your husband die in order to save the neighbor's husband or your wife, that would be altruism.

The Phil Donahue Show (1979)

PHIL DONAHUE

I'm still not sure why you're so harsh on those who would sacrifice for other people.

AYN RAND

Because they don't hesitate to sacrifice whole nations. Look at Russia—communism is based on altruism. Look at Nazi Germany—the Nazis were more explicit than even the Russians in preaching self-sacrifice and altruism, and self-sacrifice for the State, the "volk," for the people. Every dictatorship is based on altruism. Now, you can't fight it by merely saying it's a difference of opinion—it's a difference of life and death.

> *Under what social system
> is it proper for man to live?*

For the New Intellectual (1961)

(University of Michigan interview)

AYN RAND

It's the Founding Fathers who established in the United States of America the first and only free society in history. And the economic system which was the corollary of the American political system was capitalism. The system of total, unregulated, laissez-faire capitalism. This was the basic principle of the American way of life or the American political system. However, in practice it has never yet been practiced. A total separation of government and economics had not been established from the first. It was implied in principle, but certain loopholes or contradictions were still allowed into the American set-up and into the American constitution which permitted collectivist influences to undermine the American way of life. And today it is practically collapsing.

The Tomorrow Show (1979)

AYN RAND

Only, I want to make something clear. I am not a conservative. I think that today's conservatives are worse than today's liberals. I think they are . . . if anyone destroys this country, it will be the conservatives. Because they do not know how to preach capitalism, to explain it to the people. Because they do nothing except apologize and because they are all altruists. They are all based on religious altruism. And on that combination of ideas, you cannot save this country.

In spite of the pro-Soviet sentiment which surrounded the early history of *We the Living*, Ayn Rand had told America about the "Soviet cemetery." It was also against this backdrop that she had been trying desperately to get her family out of Russia.

Ayn, Frank and Mary Carr near Malibu, circa 1929.

MICHAEL S. BERLINER

"Beginning shortly after Ayn Rand came to the United States in early 1926, her family began making plans to come to the United States themselves, to emigrate—not just to visit—actually to emigrate. And they first tried to get Nora, her youngest sister, to come here. And then they began to make plans for all of them to come here. They were learning English. They said in their letters that they were speaking English at home, trying to get more used to the language. Ayn Rand herself began, in the early thirties, the process of bringing her family here after she became a citizen and was steadily employed—which was very important. She began making contact with U.S. government officials and the immigration office and the like.

"Unfortunately, under Stalin, it became virtually impossible for people to get out of Russia. So they were put in jeopardy just by corresponding with people in the West. So her family stopped writing to her—they had to—and, simultaneously, she stopped writing to them. At that time, the U.S. government was putting up notices in the post offices telling people they could endanger their families and friends just by sending them letters in Russia."

Left to Right: Ayn's Uncle Volodya Kaplan, Natasha, Ayn's father, Ayn and Ayn's mother.

CYNTHIA PEIKOFF

"The way I came across the file about her parents, I could tell that it meant a lot to her. That she tried to get them. She wanted very much to bring them over and save them because they both had medical problems that couldn't be taken care of in Russia. And I think it must have been very crushing for her to have lost them like that."

The Rosenbaum family: father, Ayn, Natasha and mother holding Nora, circa 1912.

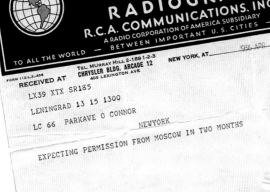

EXPECTING PERMISSION FROM MOSCOW IN TWO MONTHS

NO ANSWER YET

CANNOT GET PERMISSION

*I*n 1937, Ayn and Frank were spending a summer in Connecticut while Frank appeared in a stock version of *Night of January 16th* at the Stoney Creek Theater. In an intense struggle to work on her next novel, *The Fountainhead*, Ayn used the solitude of the country to write. Literally "tearing her hair out"* over the plot, she took a break to complete a novelette called *Anthem*.

Originally a play she conceived in Russia, *Anthem* was a futuristic account of a world where individualism has been obliterated and the word "I" has been replaced with the word "we." It was her "hymn to man's ego," to man's absolute "self," and an account of what she believed were the true implications of all forms of collectivism.

Written in the form of a diary, the story culminates with the protagonist, Equality 7-2521, rediscovering the concept of individualism.

*Animation drawing
by Cynthia Wells
from* A Sense of Life.

Equality 7-2521

"At first, man was enslaved by the gods. But he broke their chains. Then he was enslaved by the kings. But he broke their chains. He was enslaved by his birth, by his kin, by his race. But he broke their chains. He declared to all his brothers that a man has rights which neither god nor king nor other men can take away from him, no matter what their number, for his is the right of man, and there is no right on earth above this right."

Ever since she first saw the image of an American city in a Russian movie theater at age sixteen, Ayn Rand wanted to write a story that would glorify the skyscraper as a symbol of "achievement and of life on earth."* Finally understanding American life and fully an adult, she was ready to create her ideal man.

Now a question puzzled her: she had known an ambitious secretary at RKO who was a real "Hollywood climber." She, like Ayn, took her career very seriously. But Ayn disliked everything about her and one day asked her what she wanted to achieve. The girl told her, "Here's what I want out of life. If nobody had an automobile, I would not want one. If automobiles exist and some people don't have them, I want an automobile. If some people have two automobiles, I want two automobiles." It was a shock to Ayn that a person would base their goals in life on other people's standards. As if "in a flash,"* two opposing characters of her next novel were formed.

Howard Roark, the individualistic architect, and Peter Keating, the conventional second-hander of *The Fountainhead*, were born.

LEONARD PEIKOFF

"I could not understand whether the hero of *The Fountainhead*, Howard Roark, was an idealist or was practical. My father had always brought me up to believe that you have two choices in life: idealism or practicality, and that you cannot be both. And I couldn't classify Roark as either because, obviously, he was an idealist; he wouldn't compromise; he was a man of iron integrity. And, yet, at the same time, it was shown by the logic of the events that he was the one that would make a practical success of his career. Whereas his opponents, like Keating and Toohey, are doomed to fail."

MICHAEL S. BERLINER

"When I read *The Fountainhead*, it hit me like a ton of bricks because I found out what it meant to be an individualist. And, in the character of Howard Roark, there he was. Not explained as in a philosophic treatise, but dramatized and concretized. So, that's the . . . kind of . . . the glory of Ayn Rand's fiction. You can see what the philosophy means. You can see a character and think this is what it means to act on a philosophy."

For the heroine of the novel, Ayn Rand created Dominique—the aristocratic woman who first fights against Roark but then stands by him in the end. She described Dominique as herself in a "bad mood." It was an emotional state that never lasted for more than a full day for Ayn, but one that the character of Dominique takes years to overcome.

To research *The Fountainhead*, Ayn took a job as a typist for the architect Ely Jacques Kahn in New York. Through this experience, she came to admire the work of Frank Lloyd Wright. Although she did not use Wright as a model for her hero, Howard Roark, it was the originality and daring of Wright's designs that she wanted to capture.

Book jacket photo for
The Fountainhead, *1943.*

MICHAEL S. BERLINER

"In 1937, she first wrote to Frank Lloyd Wright, trying to get a meeting with him to talk about the book and explain to him what she was going to do and to get an interview with him. And she was unsuccessful; Wright was uninterested. She tried a couple of times and had gotten nowhere, but Wright eventually read *The Fountainhead* and about a year after the book was published, wrote her a letter which began, 'Your thesis is *the* great one.'"

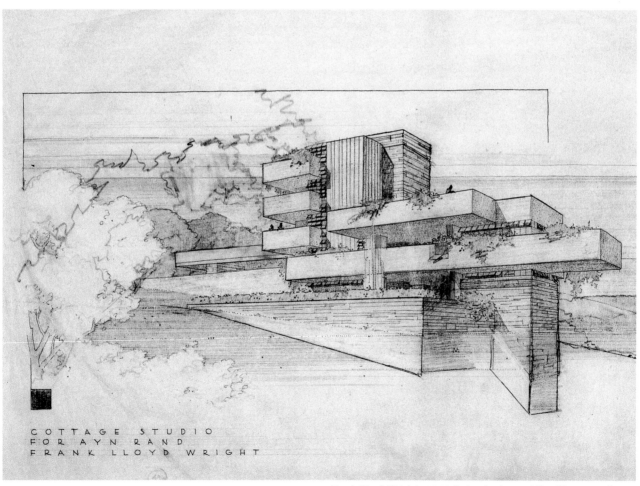

COTTAGE STUDIO
FOR AYN RAND
FRANK LLOYD WRIGHT

Frank Lloyd Wright's 1946 design for Ayn and Frank's country home.
The house was never built, because they decided to live in Manhattan.
c. 1998, The Frank Lloyd Wright Foundation

Book covers from some of Ayn Rand's fiction and nonfiction.

Ayn Rand

A yn Rand stated that the theme of *The Fountainhead* "is the issue of collectivism versus individualism not in politics but in man's soul." Rejected a total of twelve times by publishers who claimed the book would never sell, she refused to change one word of her manuscript.

She now faced the same dilemma as her own hero in *The Fountainhead*. In a key moment of the novel, a prospective client demands that Howard Roark place a classic portico on his brilliantly original design for a modern bank. Roark refuses, explaining that "an honest building, like an honest man, has to be of one piece and one faith" and that "the good, the high and the noble on earth is only that which keeps its integrity."

It was the integrity of one man at Bobbs-Merrill—Archibald Ogden—that finally got *The Fountainhead* published. Told by the head of the company to reject the book, Ogden, a new editor at the time, wrote them a note: "If this isn't the book for you, then I'm not the editor for you." Ayn signed a contract with Bobbs-Merrill, and *The Fountainhead* appeared in book stores in 1943.

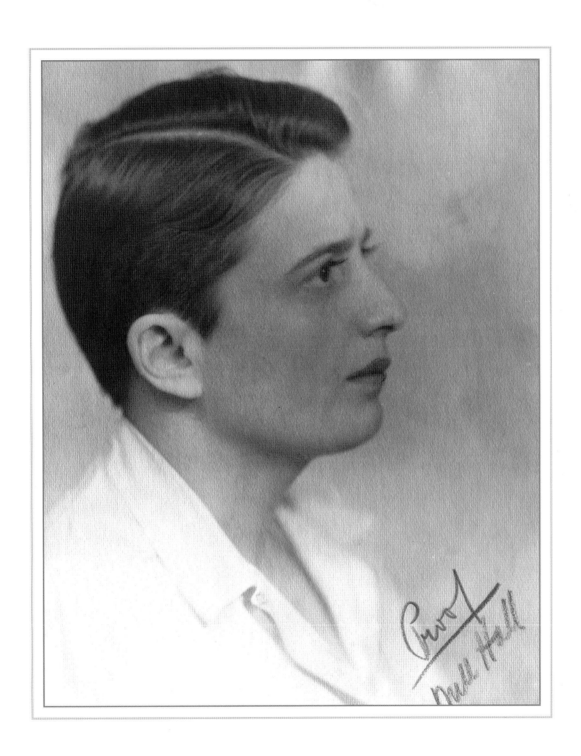

At first, to Ayn's dismay, the ad campaign never mentioned the issue of individualism versus collectivism; it focused on the love affair between Dominique and Roark. Sales of the book started out very slowly, but by 1945 it had reached the best-seller list through word of mouth, selling 100,000 copies in one year.

As *The Fountainhead*'s sales rose, Ayn was still back in New York reading scripts for Paramount while Frank struggled in the theater. Across the continent, Barbara Stanwyck, who was under contract to Warner Brothers, brought *The Fountainhead* to the attention of producer Henry Blanke. Soon Warner Brothers had bought the movie rights for fifty thousand dollars, with Stanwyck slated to play Dominique. Blanke believed that Ayn should adapt the book for the screen, and she was hired to write the screenplay.

MICHAEL S. BERLINER

"In 1943, Ayn Rand moved back to Hollywood to write *The Fountainhead* movie script. . . . She wrote to Archie Ogden, her much-beloved *Fountainhead* editor: 'As to the working conditions of a Hollywood writer's life, they are exactly as one would imagine a Hollywood writer's life—with all the trimmings. I have an office the size of a living room with another office outside and a secretary in it. Nobody can come in without being announced by my secretary, and she answers the phone. The grandeur and the glamour and the pomp and the circumstance are simply wonderful. Of course, I love it—for the moment. But I won't exchange it for the pleasure of writing as I please. I haven't gone Hollywood yet.'"

THE FOUNTAINHEAD

AYN RAND

A daring, powerful, challenging story — now a superb movie!

Your Enrollment Gift **THE FOUNTAINHEAD**, *by Ayn Rand*

Although Howard Roark was expelled from architectural school, he became the greatest architect of his generation. Nothing could swerve him from his chosen path, not even his hunger for the beautiful, brilliant Dominique. Perhaps that is why he was hated and loved—because he needed no one, depended on no one, wanted no one, and to others such a man is a challenge and a danger. A powerful, gripping modern novel which tells the story of a fascinating and formidable man—a timely expression of an impassioned faith in the individual. (Publisher's list price $3.00.)

TWO BOLD, STIRRING, UNFORGETTABLE NOVELS
A $6.00 VALUE PAY ONLY $1.00...
(AT PUBLISHERS' LIST PRICES)
for "My Son and Heir" and get *both* books

Your First Club Selection

MY SON AND HEIR, *by Isabella Holt*

A rich and dramatic chronicle of an American family's rise to wealth and power. Led by spirited, redheaded Joanna, who took her orders only from God, the Wicklund clan climbed to enviable peaks, but the changing tides of our century buffeted their stronghold and swept Joanna's son Alec into conflicts he couldn't escape. Even the two women who loved him most couldn't save him. Only a crisis which almost destroyed him—and all Joanna stood for—revealed the truth he needed and gave him the courage to face it. A magnificent, beautifully written story which is deeply moving. (Publisher's list price $3.00.)

MY SON AND HEIR

ISABELLA HOLT

Living room of house designed in 1935 by Richard Neutra and purchased by Ayn and Frank in 1944. The house was demolished in 1972.
Courtesy of Julius Shulman

*A*rriving in Hollywood, Ayn and Frank moved into a furnished apartment that didn't allow pets. After their beloved cat was discovered by the landlady, they decided to buy a house. Although hesitant of living so far from Hollywood, they found a boldly modern, thirteen-acre ranch designed by Richard Neutra in Chatsworth, California.

Frank and Ayn at Neutra house, 1947.
Courtesy of Julius Shulman

Exterior of Neutra house.
Courtesy of Julius Shulman

Now there was plenty of room for Ayn to write and for Frank to grow flowers and vegetables, which he turned into a commercial enterprise. They were also able to raise peacocks and house a few more cats.

orld War II rationing of building materials forced *The Fountainhead* movie to be put on hold due to the demands of the film's sets. Fortunately, Ayn had met producer Hal Wallis on the Warner lot, and he hired her to rewrite the love scenes in a troubled film called *The Conspirators*. She adapted two other scripts for Wallis: one was *Love Letters*, which was directed by William Dieterle and earned Jennifer Jones an Oscar® nomination in 1945. The other was the popular *You Came Along*, starring Bob Cummings and Lizabeth Scott.

Three years into her contract with Hal Wallis, she was asked to write a script about the making of the atom bomb, called "Top Secret." After completing a large portion of the script, Hal Wallis sold the project out from under her to MGM. For Ayn, it was the end of her contract with Hal Wallis and the beginning of another battle to combat collectivism.

On the set of Love Letters. *Left to right: Jennifer Jones, Hal Wallis, Ayn, director William Dieterle and Joseph Cotton, 1945.*

Ayn had been consistently disillusioned with American politics. In 1940, while volunteering on behalf of the Wendell Wilkie presidential campaign, she saw many conservatives betray the principles of individualism and capitalism. In an effort to counteract the New Deal, she stood on the stage of the Gloria Swanson Theater in New York—through seven shows a day—answering questions from the audience about the evils of collectivism. She was also voted onto the board of the Motion Picture Alliance for the Preservation of American Ideals, better known as the MPA. A conservative group formed at MGM by Louis B. Mayer, it included such Hollywood professionals as Walt Disney, Hedda Hopper, Gary Cooper, John Wayne, and Lela Rogers (Ginger's mother). Ayn was the only member to write signed articles concerning communist propaganda in the movies. Not intended as a government-imposed regulation, her pamphlet, entitled "Screen Guide for Americans," was a voluntary guide for filmmakers to monitor communist propaganda in their movies. Displeased with the MPA's fear that her ideas in the "Screen Guide" were too harsh, she resigned from the board.

In 1947, after the House Committee on Un-American Activities had read the "Guide," she was asked to testify as a "friendly witness." Along with Robert Taylor, Adolph Menjou and Gary Cooper, she appeared at the hearings in Washington to investigate communist infiltration in the movies.

Considering the endeavor "a dubious undertaking,"* she agreed, upon one condition: that there would be no restrictions on her testimony. Although she was to analyze two films, she was ultimately only allowed to speak on one, *Song of Russia*. An absurdly inaccurate glamorization of Russia, she felt it was not even worthy of scrutiny. However, she wanted to set the record straight about life in the Soviet Union.

House Un-American Committee (1947)

INTERROGATOR

Don't they do things at all like Americans—don't they walk across town to visit their mother-in-law or somebody?

AYN RAND

Look, it is very hard to explain. It's almost impossible to convey to a free people what it is like to live in a totalitarian dictatorship. I can tell you a lot of details. I can never completely convince you because you are free. And it is in a way good that you don't— that you can't even conceive of what it's like. Certainly they have friends and mothers-in-law. They try to live a human life, but you understand it is totally inhuman. Now, try to imagine what it is like if you are in constant terror from morning till night, and at night you are waiting for the doorbell to ring, where you are afraid of everything and everybody. If you live in a country where human life is nothing, less than nothing—and you know it—you don't know who—when—is going to do what to you because he may have friends somewhere, where there is no law and any rights of any kind.

Ayn with conservative activitist Lela Rogers, mother of Ginger Rogers, 1951.
Courtesy Hearst Collection, University of Southern California Library

Concerned with the flood of bad press, the committee was not interested in the cold, hard facts about life under Communism. Although Ayn didn't approve of the hearings—calling them "futile"—she believed her testimony could have been an effective way to make clear what she saw as propaganda on the screen. She tried to do what she had done in *We the Living*, but, still, no one wanted to listen. Subsequently, however, her "Screen Guide" was reprinted in many newspapers—including the *New York Times Drama Section*—and the studios began to order copies of it for distribution. Also, *The Fountainhead* sales were picking up.

Many were beginning to hear what Ayn Rand had to say.

Following the war, in 1948, Gary Cooper's wife had read *The Fountainhead* and suggested he read it. Afterwards, Cooper went to Warner Brothers and signed a two-picture-per-year deal on the condition they give him *The Fountainhead*.

During the years the film was on hold, the book had been rising in sales and popularity. Many stars were now interested in playing parts in the film. Clark Gable canceled his MGM contract when he discovered they had failed to buy the book as a vehicle for him. For the role of Roark, Humphrey Bogart and Alan Ladd were considered, as well as Clifton Webb and Orson Welles for Roark's nemesis, Ellsworth Toohey.

King Vidor on the set of Street Scene, *1931.*
Courtesy of The Academy of Motion Picture Arts and Sciences

King Vidor was signed on to direct. Vidor, a maverick of early filmmaking, had done such notable films as *The Big Parade* and *The Crowd*.

Since Ayn had previously met with Barbara Stanwyck and wanted her to do the part of Dominique, she called Stanwyck and informed her the film was starting up again. Having worked with Stanwyck on *Stella Dallas*, Vidor thought she was too old and not the right type for Dominique—he didn't think she could play a "lady." He had wanted Gene Tierney or Jennifer Jones, with whom he had just worked on *Duel in the Sun*. Although Ayn had no control over the casting of the picture, Joan Crawford hosted a dinner in Ayn's honor to garner the role. Attempting to imitate Dominique's character, Crawford wore a white Adrian evening gown smothered with aquamarine jewelry. Veronica Lake told people that Ayn had written the part for her because she had Dominique's hairstyle. At last, realizing that Stanwyck was out, Ayn suggested Greta Garbo. While initially interested, Garbo met with Vidor and decided against taking the role. Then, suddenly, Bette Davis—Warner's top star—wanted the part. Davis had gained a reputation for holding up sets, changing scripts, and arguing with her leading men. Vidor and Blanke were against hiring her and Ayn threatened to walk off the picture if they did. However, Patricia Neal was under contract as a new starlet, and the studio decided to give a relative unknown the coveted role.

The studio had now officially turned its back on Barbara Stanwyck. When Ayn realized that no one had the courage to phone Stanwyck, she phoned Stanwyck personally to let her know the part had been given away. Stanwyck immediately fired off a bitter telegram to Jack Warner and abruptly ended her contract.

Publicity still of Patricia Neal, 1949.

On The Fountainhead *set, left to right: King Vidor, Gary Cooper and Edward Carrere, 1948.*
Courtesy Warner Bros.

Finally, after Ayn had met Frank Lloyd Wright, she commissioned him to design a country home for her and Frank. Although the home was never built, she was pleased that Blanke and Vidor wanted Wright to design Roark's buildings for *The Fountainhead.* However, when Wright demanded $250,000 and final approval over the script, casting, costumes and the sets, Blanke and Vidor decided against it. Ayn then recommended Kahn and Neutra, but the studio set designer, Edward Carrere, ended up with the job. Knowing that the art department was creating structurally unsound designs for Roark's buildings, Ayn suggested Vidor never hold too long on them—she knew architects would criticize the film on this count.

*N*ow, with the cast and crew firmly in place, the film went into production.

On The Fountainhead *set. Back row (left to right): Robert Douglas (Ellsworth Toohey), Kent Smith (Peter Keating), Patricia Neal (Dominque Francon), Gary Cooper (Howard Roark), Raymond Massey (Gail Wynand). Front row: Henry Blanke (producer), Ayn and King Vidor.*

MICHAEL S. BERLINER

"She wrote to her old editor, Archie Ogden, about the beginning of the shooting. And she said to him, '*The Fountainhead* movie goes into production on Monday. In fact, the company is leaving today to go on location...the first scene shot will be the quarry. . . .

"'They are going to shoot it in a local quarry near Fresno. I've seen pictures of the place and it is quite impressive. Funny, isn't it? I remember the time when that quarry was nothing but my imagination. And now it is going to be made into a physical reality. I do feel somewhat in the position of a god—since something which I made out of spirit is now going to be translated into matter.'"

Courtesy Warner Bros.

In working on the script with Vidor, Ayn became engaged in another series of battles to keep her words intact. Neither the studio nor the censors knew what to make of *The Fountainhead*, and they were ideologically intimidated by its author.

The love scenes between Roark and Dominique—which spilled over into the personal lives of Cooper and Neal—were not as much of a concern as Roark's climactic courtroom speech. The speech was to be Roark's sole defense for dynamiting a housing project he had designed that was altered without his consent.

Gary Cooper's lawyer and the Johnston office censors were concerned about the uncompromising principles of Roark's individualism. Neither were able to justify their objections, and their questions only prompted Ayn to lengthen the speech for clarity. Increased from four and a half to six and a half minutes, Cooper would now deliver the longest speech in the history of film.

Although Cooper was serious and worked very hard, he had trouble understanding and delivering the speech. Vidor asked Ayn to coach Cooper but eventually decided to shoot a cut version of the scripted speech without Ayn's knowledge. On the day the speech was shot, Ayn happened to be on the set and discovered Vidor was shooting a shorter version of the speech. Furious, she threatened Blanke that she would disassociate herself from the picture if the speech was not shot as written. Blanke returned to the set with an edict from Jack Warner: "There were to be no changes to the script on the set." It was truly unprecedented. The speech and her script were filmed without one single word being changed.

King Vidor, Ayn and Gary Cooper, 1948.
Courtesy Warner Bros.

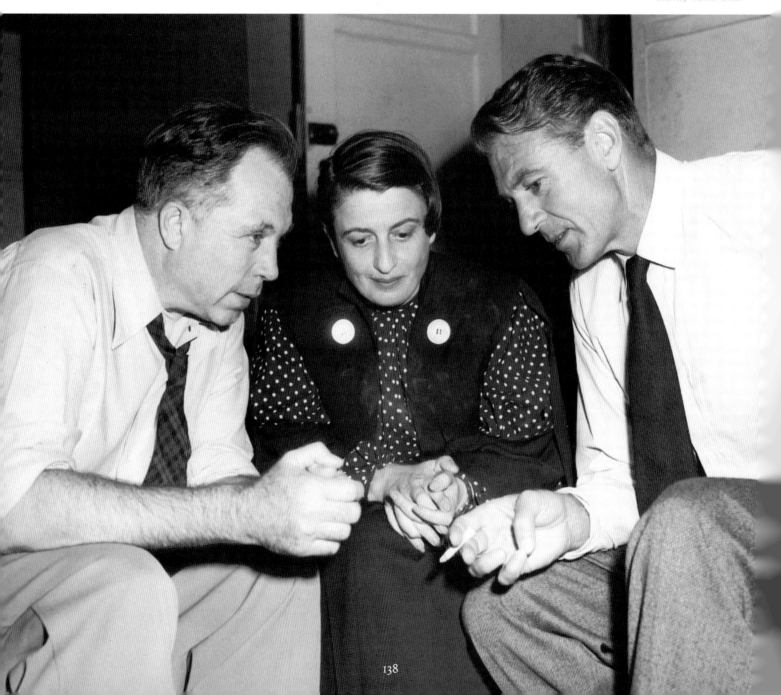

228 (Cont.)

ROARK: (Cont.)

others derived from it. The creation
which gave form to his truth. He held
his truth above all things and against
all men. He went ahead - whether others
agreed with him or not - with his integrity as his only banner. He served
nothing and no one. He lived for himself. And only by living for himself
was he able to achieve the things which
are the glory of mankind. Such is the
nature of achievement.

Man cannot survive except through his
mind. He comes on earth unarmed. His
brain is his only weapon. But the mind
is an attribute of the individual. There
is no such thing as a collective brain.

The man who thinks must think and act
on his own. The reasoning mind cannot
work under any form of compulsion. It
cannot be subordinated to the needs,
opinions or wishes of others. It is
not an object of sacrifice.

The creator stands on his own judgment.
The parasite follows the opinions of
others. The creator thinks. The
parasite copies. The creator produces.
The parasite loots. The creator's concern is the conquest of nature. The
parasite's concern is the conquest of
men.

The creator requires independence. He
neither serves nor rules. He deals
with men by free exchange and voluntary
choice. The parasite seeks power. He
wants to bind all men together in common
action and common slavery. He claims
that man is only a tool for the use of
others, that he must think as they think,
act as they act, and live in selfless,
joyless servitude to any need but his
own.

Look at history. Everything we have,
every great achievement, has come from
the independent work of some independent
mind. Every horror and destruction
came from attempts to force men into a
herd of brainless, soulless robots,
without personal ambition, without
personal rights, without will, hope or
dignity. It is an ancient conflict.

(CONTINUED)

The Fountainhead (1949)

HOWARD ROARK

Look at history. Everything we have, every great achievement, has come from the independent work of some independent mind. . . .

I came here to say that I do not recognize anyone's right to one minute of my life . . . nor to any part of my energy. Nor to any achievement of mine. No matter who makes the claim. It had to be said. The world is perishing from an orgy of self-sacrificing. I came here to be heard in the name of every man of independence still left in the world. I wanted to state my terms. I do not care to work or live on any others. My terms are: a man's right to exist for his own sake.

Shooting the courtroom scene from The Fountainhead, *1948.*

Gary Cooper as Howard Roark in the final scene from The Fountainhead, *1949.*
Courtesy Warner Bros.

LEONARD PEIKOFF

"She was proud of the script—she thought it was good and honest within the framework of their abilities, that they didn't sabotage the novel, but it wasn't what she would consider a work of art."

Ayn was disappointed that the film lacked the romanticism she so loved in the German films she had seen in her youth. But the film was a windfall as advertising for the book.

By 1961, the hardcover edition of *The Fountainhead* soared past 500,000 copies. To this day, *The Fountainhead* sells 100,000 copies annually. For a book that publishers claimed would never sell, Ayn Rand's first story projecting her ideal man was an undeniable success.

Late in 1950, Ayn Rand received a fan letter from a young psychology student, Nathaniel Branden. She thought his letter was so intelligent and his questions so astute that she invited him to call on her in person to discuss them further. Both Ayn and Frank were completely won over by him after their first meeting, and Nathaniel began seeing them more frequently. By 1953, Ayn and Frank stood up at Nathaniel's wedding and in the years that followed, the Brandens and the O'Connors formed an intimate circle.

LEONARD PEIKOFF

"Nathaniel Branden meant a great deal to Ayn Rand. She thought he was a genius, an exceptional intelligence, that he would be an innovator in the field of psychology, that he took ideas with passion and seriousness. She obviously liked him and, by all the evidence that I have, she had an affair with him, which she would not do if she didn't have the highest possible opinion of him. This she did, of course, with the knowledge of her husband and the consent of her husband. . . . I don't have any—really—inside information of how Frank coped with the knowledge of the affair. I presume there had to be some jealousy, but he was not characteristically a jealous person and I think he felt—now, I'm taking my educated guess here—I think he felt that in some way that she was uniquely special and that she needed more from a man than he could offer. And, as I see it in my own mind, Frank had the soul that Ayn Rand needed, but he didn't have the intellect. He didn't have that glowing, brilliant, intellectual's type of intellect which Branden seemed to have."

CYNTHIA PEIKOFF

"It's true—that she had great needs because of her personality. She needed both a soul mate and a certain sense of life in a man, but she also needed somebody she could talk as an intellectual to."

Nathanial Branden (upper left) and Ayn, 1960s.

Nathaniel Branden created an institute to teach a lecture series based on Ayn Rand's philosophy. Ayn endorsed his courses and the articles he wrote on psychology that appeared in magazines and books. Eventually, however, she was to discover that he was involved in a series of personal and professional deceptions.

"In my opinion, Nathaniel Branden was the supreme actor, who communicated that nothing mattered more to him than ideas. He wanted nothing from the world but the truth. And the [revelation] of the truth was all that counted. And he was an idealist and so on. And that was what he presented himself as originally. He was very intelligent. It wasn't the case of a dolt who was able to put it over. He was actually very intelligent . . . But in the course of his life, his values obviously came to change, for whatever reason, because of his preexisting psychology or whatever. He had to act an increasingly onerous part to retain Ayn's affection. Namely, to pretend something that he knew he was not and no longer wanted to be. And, finally, it became intolerable and one thing or another precipitated the break. . . . She bore it but, finally, did get over it and go on with her life of writing and with her husband."

s Ayn's writing continued, Frank O'Connor had been steadily trying to find his niche. Glowing with admiration, he enjoyed watching his wife but never tried to manage her career. He was an independent entity gracefully, quietly searching for his life's work.

HARRY BINSWANGER

"Frank was an amazing man. First of all, he looked totally like an Ayn Rand hero—he stood out in any crowd. He was, in my view, the Howard Roark type."

Frank and Leonard Peikoff, 1971.

Ayn and Frank with Gary Cooper on The Fountainhead *set, 1948.*
Courtesy Warner Bros.

LEONARD PEIKOFF

"My impression of Frank from the beginning was that he was a very fine, very sensitive artist type. He was not dominantly the talker, but you felt that he was a very strong and sensitive presence with her and then, in later years, he looked for the career that would give him full satisfaction for many years. And, finally, the logic of his choices took him into painting. And that's where he really found himself, and he began to do tremendous work. What he did always had the Frank O'Connor touch to it, that she would describe as 'laughter let loose in the universe.'"

Frank painting in his studio in New York, 1966.

Diminishing
Returns
by
Frank O'Connor,
circa 1960.

For the New Intellectual (1961)

(University of Michigan interview)

INTERVIEWER

Our Founding Fathers talked about the right of the pursuit of happiness. Do you think this is really important?

AYN RAND

I don't know what else could be any more important if you attach exact meaning to concepts. The "pursuit of happiness" means a man's right to set his own goals, to choose his values and to achieve them. Happiness means that state of consciousness which comes from the achievement of your values. Now, what can be more important than happiness? But happiness does not mean, simply, momentary pleasures or any kind of mindless self-indulgence. Happiness means a profound, guiltless, rational feeling of self-esteem and of pride in one's own achievement. It means the enjoyment of life which is possible only to a rational man on a rational code of morality.

The Tomorrow Show (1979)

AYN RAND

Because to make a success of yourself in any line of rational activity·is a great virtue, and . . . they . . . people will attack you for exercising your ability for hard work, for consistency, for ambition. And they will want to make you feel guilty of it . . . in fact, people who preach that are the ones who are mawkish about the evil people—the failures, the liars, the cheats. Everybody who is weak suddenly acquires some kind of value. But anyone who is a success has to be attacked for his success.

TOM SNYDER

And look at how you have been attacked . . .

AYN RAND

Oh, I know . . .

TOM SNYDER

How you have been criticized . . .

AYN RAND

You know that?

TOM SNYDER

There are many people in this country, forgive me—in this world—who think you're daft!

AYN RAND

They don't. They want you to think that.

uring *The Fountainhead*'s rise to the top, Ayn and Frank had been happy at the Chatsworth ranch. But Ayn had grown weary of the country and living in California. She missed New York.

Ayn and Frank, patio of Neutra house, 1947.

MICHAEL S. BERLINER,
(*reading a letter from Ayn Rand*)

"'I hate Hollywood as a place just as I did before. It's overcrowded, vulgar, cheap, and sad in a hopeless sort of way. The people on the streets are all tense, eager and suspicious and look unhappy. The has-beens and the would-be's. I'm in love with New York. Frank says that what I love is not the real city, but the New York I built myself. That's true.'"

LEONARD PEIKOFF

"New York represented, to her, the pinnacle of human achievement in physical terms. Aristotle would be the pinnacle of achievement intellectually. But New York—the skyscrapers, everything that man had traversed from the time of the cave till the time of this glorious and industrial civilization—that was, to her, what life was about. It wasn't just acquiring philosophy, it was acquiring ideas and science and then remaking the earth accordingly, and she couldn't think of a more splendid and exciting and beautiful place than that view that you get of the skyscrapers where you don't see the details of each one, but the mass of human ingenuity and talent soaring from the sky."

Daniel E. Greene's portrait of Ayn Rand, 1960.
Courtesy Harry Binswanger

DANIEL E. GREENE

"I took a studio in New York in a very seedy old hotel on Thirty-first, and Ayn came to pose for me there. There were no windows in the studio, but there was a skylight, and the only thing one could see from the skylight was the top of the Empire State Building. And Ayn was particularly smitten with that. I subsequently moved to Greenwich Village, and she came down there to pose as well. And the atmosphere was a little different. I think she wasn't quite as happy in that studio as she was being able to see the Empire State Building while she posed."

In 1951, Ayn and Frank moved to New York City—the city she had first seen as a backdrop of electric lights in a Russian theater. Now, as a successful American writer, she would live in one of that city's skyscrapers. And here she would complete her monumental book, *Atlas Shrugged*.

When a friend insisted Ayn write a nonfiction treatise on her philosophy out of a duty to help people understand her ideas, she was indignant. She thought, "Why should I? What if I went on strike? What if all the creative minds of the world went on strike?"

Animation drawings by Cynthia Wells from A Sense of Life.

Hence, the story of men and women of the mind who go on strike and abandon the world was formed. Wider in scope than *The Fountainhead, Atlas Shrugged* dramatized the whole of Ayn Rand's philosophy, allowing Ayn to express her total sense of life—a life she knew could and should exist. Likening the new heroes in the book to the giant Greek god who supported the heavens on his shoulders, Ayn focused on three captains of industry—a copper magnate, a steel mill owner and the head of a railroad. They were the creators, innovators and independent thinkers who moved the world but decided to "shrug." She told a reporter at the time that the story would "combine metaphysics, morality, politics, economics and sex. . . ." And, as she had promised her professor in Russia, the book would finally make her ideas a part of the history of philosophy.

As the mystery story of *Atlas Shrugged* unfolds, Ayn Rand erects an unprecedented argument for capitalism. Presenting a moral defense for man's right to exist for his own sake, to pursue the work of his choice, and to keep the rewards of his labor, she argued that "capitalism demands the best of every man—his rationality—and rewards him accordingly. It leaves every man free to choose the work he likes, to specialize in it, to trade his product for the products of others, and to go as far on the road of achievement as his ability and ambition will carry him."

Billboard in Georgia, 1967.

"Who is John Galt?" was the burning question that opened *Atlas Shrugged*. Although Frank posed in publicity ads for the book, Galt was a direct descendant of Cyrus in *The Mysterious Valley*. Like Cyrus, Galt was a hero operating behind the scenes for a good portion of the story. The heroine, Dagny Taggart, the driving force behind Taggart Transcontinental Railroad, was Ayn's first depiction of an ideal woman, a character she called "the feminine Roark."

Ayn herself read manuals on railroad signal switching and steel furnaces. She visited the Kaiser Steel mills in California, as well as other mills in Chicago and Johnstown. She researched all the major railroads and eventually interviewed people from the New York Central. Bobbs-Merrill, the publisher of *The Fountainhead*, arranged a trip for her on the *Twentieth Century* to Albany from New York City. A particular thrill for her was when the engineer allowed her to drive the train herself.

Ayn traveling by train, 1947.

Frank, their cat Frisco and Ayn, 1950s.

Ayn, after returning to New York, in an apartment decorated by Frank, 1951.

The demands of writing the novel took all of her energy and focus. She often worked many hours at a time, stopping only to eat or cook a meal for Frank. Often she would lose all track of time, and they would end up having supper at ten or eleven o'clock at night. When she was stuck or had what she called, "the squirms," she would take a break to play solitaire or visit with friends.

Ayn with Leonard Peikoff, 1960s.

LEONARD PEIKOFF

"Well, there was a group of us, around ten or twelve who were related—either one was a friend of another or a relative of another. And, as a joke, Ayn started to call us 'The Collective.' As a joke, because we were all supposed to be arch individualists. . . . We came to her place on a regular basis, starting originally on Saturday nights, to read the manuscript of *Atlas Shrugged*, and then we would read whatever was available or some given chapter, and then there would be an all-around discussion monitored by her. And then she would serve something around midnight or one in the morning—sometimes we would stay till three or four in the morning. And, at first, we got to know her best through these weekly Saturday-night sessions."

ow, her biggest challenge was writing Galt's climactic speech, which he delivers to a collapsing world over radio airwaves. Thinking it would take roughly three months to complete Galt's speech, Ayn ultimately spent two years perfecting it. It encompassed her entire philosophy, which she later called Objectivism. When she finished the speech, she submitted the book to publishers. With little bargaining, she signed a contract at Random House for a fifty-thousand-dollar advance to finish the book. It was the fastest contract she ever signed.

Book jacket portrait for Atlas Shrugged, *1957.*
Photo by Phyllis Cerf

Photo by Phyllis Cerf

ver since *Atlas Shrugged* had been completed in March 1957, Ayn felt as if she were basking in the glow of her own sun. Standing back on the horizon, she was happy to simply contemplate her achievement. But when her eyes adjusted to the muted light of the world around her, she observed the current state of the culture—from the war in Vietnam and student unrest to what she termed "the anti-industrial revolution." She had been so full of the sense of life in her novels, the world of the 1960s now seemed like the "last days of the Roman Empire."* Review after review of *Atlas Shrugged* viciously attempted to discredit her and her work. But however much the attacks in the press hurt her, they only stoked the fire that would bring her out into the public.

Courtesy Playboy Magazine

LEONARD PEIKOFF

"She did not like public speaking. She did not regard herself as a teacher by
profession or by interest. She thought her accent was wrong—as far as public
speaking—and she'd never been able to do much with her accent. But she
would be damned if she was going to let *Atlas Shrugged* be commented on
exclusively by the critics who hated it; she got invitations, so she made up her
mind that despite all her reservations, she was going to speak at least enough
to give it some publicity. So, she went reluctantly. She faced, at first, very
antagonistic audiences. They booed her, they tried to out-yell her, but, of
course, she was immutable—she was herself on the lecture platform. And I've
seen audiences start booing and end up cheering."

HARRY BINSWANGER

"She had the ability to deal with anything that could come up from an audience. That was very impressive. I can't tell you what a contrast it made to the sense of life of the period. We were just coming out of the fifties, the *Leave It To Beaver, Father Knows Best* era—when no one would take a stand on anything, when making a value-judgment was considered a sin. But she was there making the most dramatic and passionate statements, saying [that] everything was simple, absolute, clear."

SYLVIA BOKOR

"She took time to find out what you had on your mind. And, oftentime [sic]—in lectures at Ford Hall Forum, where there were hundreds of people in the audience—she would still take her time. She'd say, 'Would you care to repeat that? Would you care to rephrase that so I understand what you're getting at?' That's what impressed me most."

LEONARD PEIKOFF

"She not only answered the question, she told you what errors you made that led you to that question, why you weren't able to answer it yourself, what confusions would arise tomorrow when you thought over her answers, and what the answers to those were. And, then, what to read to consolidate your thinking even more clearly. So, it was like an entire course. It wasn't just 'yes' or 'no' answer[s]. Every question was a springboard to a total exploration of the issue and of the proper methods of thinking."

JOHN RIDPATH

"When Ayn Rand appeared annually at the Ford Hall Forum, it attracted a very large crowd. She would go to a room after she had given her talk. People would line up in a very crowded little room. There weren't all the books available on her philosophical thoughts to us, so, needless to say, we would build up a huge inventory of puzzling questions since the last time we met her, and she would just field questions until dawn—at which time she was thoroughly relaxed—and she had come down from the excitement of the talk, and she would say good night to us, and we would walk out so revved up that in one case I couldn't go to sleep for two days after I had left her hotel room."

The Phil Donahue Show (1979)

PHIL DONAHUE

I know many of you have heard this line, "*Atlas Shrugged* changed my life. . . . *The Fountainhead* changed my life." Here is a woman who's read by millions around the world. She may be our most debated philosopher. She identifies that to which she adheres as Objectivism. We'll talk about it. We care very much about your sharing with us your feelings about this most interesting lady, a warm human being who has a lot to say and comes straight at everything she says. I am pleased to present Ayn Rand . . . Miss Rand.

AL RAMRUS

"The first show that Ayn Rand appeared on for us was *The Mike Wallace Interview*, and, for all I know, it was certainly one of the first shows she appeared on in the fifties, if not the very first show. She was not very welcomed. She was a notorious figure in New York intellectual circles, and it's hard now, in the nineties, to imagine the hostility directed at her. Saul Bellow once said that New York at that time was an intellectual annex of Moscow. And if it was that for Saul Bellow, you can imagine what it was like for Ayn Rand."

MIKE WALLACE

"The people I worked with simply wanted me to do a piece with Ayn Rand, and I didn't know a lot about her. I had read *The Fountainhead*, and I'm not certain— I don't remember, because I read it later—whether I had yet read *Atlas Shrugged*. And so I didn't meet her until she came into the studio."

The Mike Wallace Interview (1959)

MIKE WALLACE

This is Mike Wallace with another television portrait from our gallery of colorful people. Throughout the United States, small pockets of intellectuals have become involved in a new and unusual philosophy that would seem to strike at the very roots of our society. The fountainhead of this philosophy is a novelist, Ayn Rand, whose two major works— *The Fountainhead* and *Atlas Shrugged*—have been best-sellers. We'll try to find out more about her revolutionary creed and about Miss Rand herself in just a moment.

MIKE WALLACE

"Dark, black. That Dutch cut. Those piercing Russian eyes—strange-looking person. And the accent."

AL RAMRUS

"The first thing that struck you when you met Ayn Rand for the first time were those eyes. Big, black, glowing, lustrous eyes which radiated a tremendous energy and penetration and focus and intensity. And they never left you. And it was very unnerving—at least to me—at first. You got used to it somewhat, but, at first, it was unnerving and, perhaps, even a little intimidating."

MIKE WALLACE

"And she would take any question. She was perfectly open and you could see the mind at work and the spirit at work, and she liked the joust of tough questions and direct answers."

The Mike Wallace Interview (1959)

AYN RAND

My morality is based on man's life as a standard of value. And since man's mind is his basic means of survival, I hold that if man wants to live on earth and to live as a human being, he has to hold reason as his only guide to action and that he must live by the independent judgment of his own mind. That his highest moral purpose is the achievement of his own happiness, and that he must not force other people nor accept their right to force him. That each man must live as an end in himself and follow his own rational self-interest.

AL RAMRUS

"She was obviously the most unusual guest we ever had. You just didn't get guests who could speak for a half hour about philosophy and ideas clearly, penetratingly, and excitingly. And we would get enormous mail. I would, afterwards, get into big arguments and fights with my other friends in the media. 'Why did you put her on?' 'How could you do such a thing?' And it's very interesting: these were documentarians and writers and news people, all of whom would argue very vociferously against Ayn Rand—none of them had ever read her works and, to my knowledge, none of them ever have. As if they were afraid somehow of being stripped of their illusions—they'd rather cling to them."

In an outline for a new novel, Ayn chose a dancer named Hella as her heroine. Hella wants to create a new form of dance, one that combines the rhythmic precision of tap with the graceful elegance of ballet. "The real essence of the story," Ayn wrote in notes to herself, "is to be the universe of my tiddlywink music, of my sense of life."

But the state of the culture made it impossible for her to complete another novel. She was no longer able to project her type of heroes into the world she was now living.

By 1961, she thought that many Americans had given up on finding solutions to their problems—they were cynical and scared. Despite this, she still believed in their sense of life. She was also convinced that the young had not yet been corrupted by her critics or the intellectuals. As *Atlas Shrugged* rose in sales and on the best-seller lists, Ayn began to make more and more television appearances—from *The Merv Griffin Show* to *The Tonight Show* with Johnny Carson.

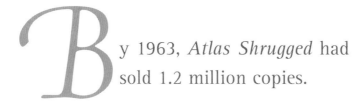

By 1963, *Atlas Shrugged* had sold 1.2 million copies.

January 2, 1964

"To Lorne Ditterling"

<u>Theme</u>: Loyalty to values, <u>as a sense of life</u>.

My earlier notes are all wrong. The approach I projected is too intellectual - too explicit. The novel has to deal with the generalized terms of a "sense of life" - i.e., with <u>emotional</u> metaphysics. The nature of the assignment (and the trick) is to <u>concretize</u> <u>the story, while keeping it abstract</u>.

This is why Hella has to be a dancer. Convey the meaning of music and dancing, as the esthetic expression of a "sense of life."

Notes regarding the dancer, Hella, from Ayn's unwritten novel "To Lorne Dieterling."

For the New Intellectual (1961)

(University of Michigan interview)

INTERVIEWER

Do you consider yourself primarily a novelist or primarily a philosopher?

AYN RAND

I would say I'm primarily both, equally and for the same reasons. You see, my main interest and purpose both in literature and philosophy is to define and present the image of an ideal man—the specific, complete image of what man can be and ought to be—and when I started writing, when I approached the task of literature and began to study philosophy, I discovered that I was in profound disagreement with all the existing philosophies—particularly their codes of morality. Therefore, I had to do my own thinking. I had to define my own philosophical system in order to discover and present the kind of ideas and premises that make an ideal man possible—in order to define what kind of convictions would result in the character of an ideal man.

Presidents' Advanced Round Table, AMA Grove Lake Moraine, Hamilton, New York, October 2-6, 1961.

Through conversations with Leonard Peikoff, Ayn saw that many of her philosophic principles were not self-evident to those around her. She realized a more detailed elaboration of her philosophy was needed. Now that Howard Roark, John Galt and Dagny Taggart existed, she had accomplished what she had set out to do in fiction and was ready to begin writing in the field of philosophy.

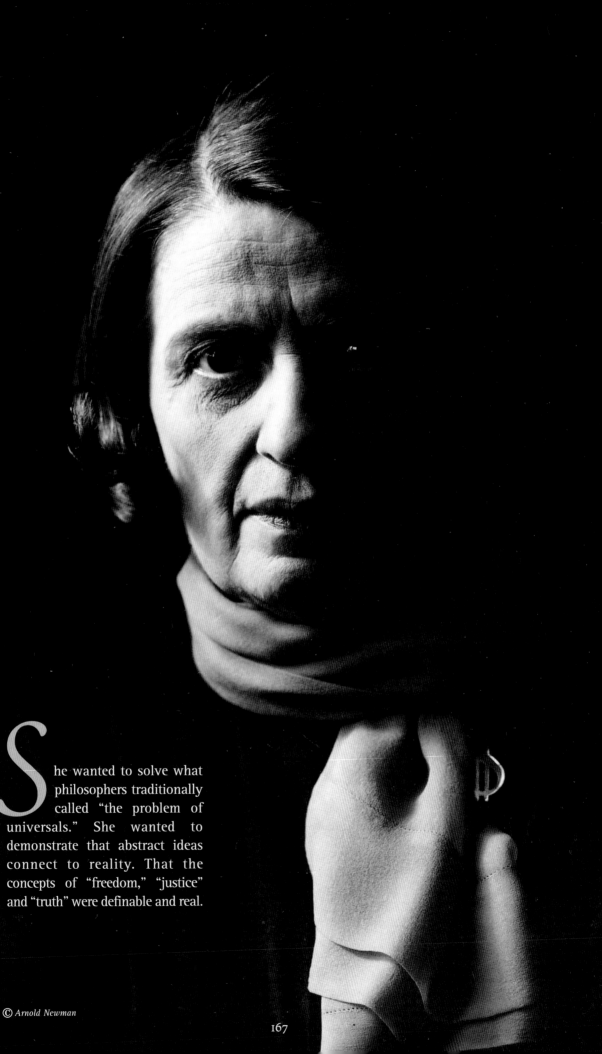

She wanted to solve what philosophers traditionally called "the problem of universals." She wanted to demonstrate that abstract ideas connect to reality. That the concepts of "freedom," "justice" and "truth" were definable and real.

HARRY BINSWANGER

"Leonard Peikoff put it to me this way, in regard to the way that she used ideas. He said, 'You know the way you or I hold the concept chair? Well, that's the way she holds the highest, deepest, philosophical abstraction—with that same kind of clarity and concreteness.' I think that's the secret of her method—that her ideas were always derived from reality, for the purpose of living in reality. That's why they were so urgently important for her. They were not a game. They were for the purpose of living her life and achieving her values."

LEONARD PEIKOFF

"I asked her once—when I was much younger—why she got so emotionally upset at the theories of philosophers like Immanuel Kant. And she said to me, 'Because when I hear a philosopher say there is no reality and your mind is totally invalid, that means all of your values are nullified: your husband, your love, your work, the music you like, your freedom.' It was truly a life-and-death matter to her. She thought philosophy moved the world, and if anybody has confusion about a philosophic issue, that could be a peril to their soul, their cognition, their clarity. She hears the total destruction in the abstract statement. Most people hear abstractions as, simply, floating abstractions. But, for her, she translated it into the actual, concrete things that it meant and what it would mean in her own life. And she was able to react emotionally to broad abstractions which very few people can do."

The Tomorrow Show (1979)

TOM SNYDER

When did you discover or think up or allow Objectivism to become your philosophy?

AYN RAND

From the time that I remember myself—which is two and a half. The first incident in my life I remember . . . I was two and a half and from that time on to the present, I never changed my convictions. Only at two and a half I didn't know as much as I know now, but the fundamental approach was the same. I've never had to change it.

TOM SNYDER

Why has it worked for you?

AYN RAND

Because it's true. Because it corresponds to reality. Because it is the right philosophy. By "true," I mean it corresponds to reality. Therefore, it permits me to deal with reality properly.

Throughout the sixties and seventies, Ayn continued to articulate her philosophy through various interviews and articles. Without a border to get beyond or an artistic purpose burning inside of her, she now had a new reason to work and a new forum to operate in. Along with publishing books on epistemology, ethics, social philosophy, and aesthetics, she also launched various philosophical magazines. She wanted to create what she described as a "*Readers Digest* for the man of intellect and action." And, to her surprise, she enjoyed the process.

She once wrote, "Do you know that my personal crusade in life (in the philosophical sense) is not merely to fight collectivism, nor to fight altruism? These are only consequences, effects, not causes. I am out after the real cause, the real root of evil on earth—the irrational."

Photo by Phyllis Cerf

*I*n interviews and articles, Ayn applied the essence of her philosophy to a variety of topics:

Upon the death of Marilyn Monroe, Ayn wrote that the beloved star had projected "the sense of a person born and reared in some radiant Utopia, untouched by suffering, unable to conceive of ugliness or evil, facing life with confidence, the benevolence and the joyous self-flaunting of a child or a kitten who is happy to display its own attractiveness as the best gift it can offer the world. . . . To preserve that kind of spirit . . . on the screen—the radiantly benevolent sense of life, which cannot be faked—was an almost inconceivable psychological achievement that required a heroism of the highest order."

In her book *The Virtue of Selfishness*, Ayn wrote that "racism is a doctrine of, by and for brutes. It is a barnyard or stock-farm version of collectivism, appropriate to a mentality that differentiates between various breeds of animals, but not between animals and men. Like every form of determinism, racism invalidates the specific attribute which distinguishes man from all other living species: his rational faculty."

In 1969, after Ayn and Frank were invited to attend the launching of *Apollo 11*, she wrote, "One knew that this spectacle was not the product of inanimate nature, like some aurora borealis, nor of chance, nor of luck, that it was unmistakably human—with *human*, for once, meaning 'grandeur.'"

PHIL DONAHUE

Religion or the god concept or faith or worship has people . . . has people thinking of life as a veil of tears through which . . .

AYN RAND

That's right . . .

PHIL DONAHUE

. . . you will probably not get without falling. You are essentially an evil person who is bent toward . . .

AYN RAND

Well, most religions do preach just that.

PHIL DONAHUE

And you don't believe that?

AYN RAND

God, no!

PHIL DONAHUE

We are here and we should celebrate it, use it, enjoy it, be selfish . . .

AYN RAND

Right.

PHIL DONAHUE

There's a virtue in selfishness . . .

AYN RAND

Right.

PHIL DONAHUE

. . . and we got ourselves in trouble when we started using government to force us to be good—because we had this notion that we had a sort of bad nature . . .

AYN RAND

Right. And if we have a bad nature, we have no self-esteem. If we have no self-esteem, any demagogue can have us. He can order us about because we wouldn't consider ourselves valuable enough to be free. You would be anxious to follow anyone because you don't trust yourself.

Ayn's sister Nora.

The gulf between Ayn Rand and the Soviet Union had made it impossible for her to know what had happened to her family. After permission to bring them to America had been denied, she had given up any hope of ever seeing them again. In 1973, Ayn's youngest sister, Nora, saw an article in Russia about the now-famous author Ayn Rand. She wrote to Ayn, and they began a renewed correspondence.

Through Nora's letters, Ayn learned that her youngest sister had become a professional set designer. Ayn also learned that her parents had since died of illnesses under Stalin and her sister Natasha had been killed in a park during an air raid in World War II.

As difficult as it was to accept these facts, Ayn focused on her joy at finding Nora, and she immediately began to make arrangements to bring her to America. In a letter to Nora she wrote, "A long time has passed, but I was hoping that you would know or feel that I have not forgotten you and never will. I have always dreamt that I would see you some day." In anticipation of Nora's arrival, Ayn rented an apartment in her building in New York and decorated it with Nora's colorful paintings.

After almost fifty years between them, Nora finally arrived, and Ayn was overjoyed. But soon she discovered Nora had become a very different person. Although Nora claimed to be an anticommunist, she complained about the futility of life and, indeed, had long given in to that concept. The sense of life Ayn had shared with Nora in their youth had been suffocated. After a few days in New York, Nora openly declared that she didn't like America or Ayn's novels. Soon the sisters were not speaking to one another. Eventually, even though Nora's husband was seriously ill and could not secure proper medical care in Russia, they returned to the Soviet Union.

Ayn's sister Nora, 1930s.

Nora with her husband Fedor Drobyshev.

Ayn watched the one person to whom she had had a meaningful bond in her childhood walk away from her—and walk willingly into an old prison. But she herself had fought so many years to survive, it was inconceivable to her to give in to the tragedy of Nora's fate. To Ayn, suffering could never be considered important.

Ayn's passport photo, 1925.

"One feels certain that somewhere on earth—
even if not anywhere in one's surroundings or
within one's reach—a proper, human
way of life is possible to human beings,
and justice matters."

From "Inexplicable Personal Alchemy" in The New Left *by Ayn Rand, p.118.*

The Tomorrow Show (1979)

TOM SNYDER

You love this country, don't you?

AYN RAND

Passionately. Very, very much and consciously. I love it for its ideas. And I've seen enough of the other side, so I can appreciate this country.

TOM SNYDER

You might even get emotional about this country.

AYN RAND

Oh, yes! You want me to get emotional?

TOM SNYDER

Might even thank God for it?

AYN RAND

Yeah . . . I may not literally mean a "god," but I like what that expression means: "thank God" or "God bless you." It means the highest possible to me and I would certainly thank God for this country.

By 1978, Frank had begun to show signs of arterial sclerosis. Soon he would have episodes of memory loss and disorientation. Earlier, Ayn had her own bout with illness. A surgery to remove a cancerous lesion from her lung had forced her to stop smoking. Yet, even while convalescing, she kept a vigil, hoping that Frank would recover.

LEONARD PEIKOFF

"I had the privilege of attending her fiftieth-anniversary party when her husband was still pretty much oriented and functionable. . . . But it was one of the very last times that he could appear in public. It was wonderful to see them together and everybody made speeches about, you know, how their love had endured fifty years."

HARRY BINSWANGER

"The relationship between Ayn and Frank was very noticeable, because here was this couple married fifty years, always holding hands. She would always say when he came into the room, 'Hello, Darlink,' with that Russian accent. She didn't want to be away from him for a second, and he felt the same way. The affection was quite noticeable. A lot of endearments. You know, she called him 'cubbyhole.' His pet name for her was 'kitten fluff.' But it was quite affectionate."

Ayn and Frank in Chatsworth, 1947.
Courtesy Julius Shulman

Frank and Ayn on New Year's Eve, 1967.

In November of 1979, not long after their fiftieth wedding anniversary, Frank's life came to an end at the age of eighty-two.

Ayn and Frank at their home in Chatsworth.

HARRY BINSWANGER

"She was crushed. She wouldn't show anything outwardly. She told me once that she was like a lion. That when she was hurt she wanted to crawl off in solitude—hurt or sick—crawl off in solitude and not show her suffering to anyone else. But you could see the absence of fire in her."

CYNTHIA PEIKOFF

"I think when she lost Frank, she basically lost her will to live. I thought she was depressed after that. She didn't have much energy. She didn't really want to go places. But she managed to keep going."

yn Rand once wrote that "it is with a person's sense of life that one falls in love—with that essential sum, that fundamental stand or way of facing existence, which is the essence of a personality." Now, that personality was gone.

The Phil Donahue Show (1980)

PHIL DONAHUE

Does this emotional impact of this kind of pain alter in any way your own feeling—philosophy?

AYN RAND

No. It only altered my position in regard to the world. Which is that I lost my top value—I'm not too interested in anything else. But I'll survive it because I do love the world in general and I do love ideas . . .

PHIL DONAHUE

Yes . . .

AYN RAND

. . . and I do love man but . . .

PHIL DONAHUE

I know. Isn't there a temptation for you—and I don't mean this to . . . [sound] . . . flip . . . to suggest that you're not sincere in your writings—to hope for a reunion with the person you love? To look beyond the . . .

AYN RAND

I've asked myself just that—seriously. And I thought that if I really believed that for five minutes, I'd commit suicide immediately and I know that cannot be right.

PHIL DONAHUE

In other words, you'd get to him right away . . .

AYN RAND

To get to him, of course. I'll tell you more. I asked myself, how would I feel if I think he's now on trial before God or Saint Peter and I'm not there . . .

PHIL DONAHUE

To testify or to help him out . . .

AYN RAND

Exactly! My first desire in that case would be to run and help him and tell how good he was.

"There are two aspects of man's existence which are the special province and expression of his sense of life," she wrote, ". . . love and art." With Frank no longer beside her, Ayn's depression intensified. But, as with all tragedy and Ayn Rand, it could not completely stifle her enthusiasm for living. After several attempts to bring *Atlas Shrugged* to the television and movie screens, she decided to write and produce her own filmed version of the book. Recovering somewhat from the loss of Frank, she had a renewed sense of purpose.

In spite of her failing health, she gave a speech in New Orleans in 1981 and announced her plans to make *Atlas Shrugged* into a miniseries.

JOHN RIDPATH

"She gave a lecture on the natural connection between the philosopher and the businessman and tried to open their eyes to the fact that, as she did in *Atlas Shrugged*, that they were—by ignoring philosophy—financing their own demise."

LEONARD PEIKOFF

"Well, she agreed to speak in New Orleans because Jim Blanchard, the man who was sponsoring the conference—National Conference on Monetary Reform, I believe—offered her what she had always wanted: a private train."

JOHN RIDPATH

"Leonard Peikoff and I escorted her from her hotel suite back to the railroad car because . . . she wanted to—I think they were leaving early in the morning and she wanted to go to sleep on the car rather than in the hotel. . . . And that's the last time I saw her. She was showing us the railroad car. She had such a capacity for the delight of all of the wonderful things man could make. The fact that she could travel on a railroad car in such sumptuous comfort and it was just a total delight for her."

LEONARD PEIKOFF

"Unfortunately, she took ill on the train coming back. And she realistically never recovered. Her faculties were still good at the end. A night or so before she died, some new cover copy for one of her forthcoming books came from the publisher, and she went over it with me and told them what to change and so on. And then, as was expected, she just slipped away."

AL RAMRUS

"I once spent part of an evening alone with Ayn Rand, talking, and somehow the subject of death came up. And I asked her if she was afraid of dying. And she said, 'No, death is insignificant and unimportant. Eternity is important. And eternity is now.' I'll never forget that."

The Tomorrow Show (1979)

TOM SNYDER

I kind of think of this whole thing as ongoing—that there is an eternity and that we're going to be a part of that eternity. That we're not just corpses in graves when we die.

AYN RAND

But we aren't corpses in graves. We are not there. Don't you understand that when this life is finished, you're not there to say, "Oh, how terrible that I'm a corpse." No.

TOM SNYDER

Well, this is true.

AYN RAND

It's finished. And what I've always thought was a sentence from some Greek philosopher—I don't unfortunately remember who it was—that I read at sixteen and it's affected me all my life: "I will not die; it's the world that will end." And that's absolutely true. And you know for me now, it should be a serious question because my time is fairly limited. And I have the same feeling that I will enjoy life to the last moment and when it's the end I don't have to worry about it. I'm not there. It's too bad that the world will end—and I think a very wonderful world will end with me, but I've had my time and I can't complain.

Ayn Rand died at her home from heart failure on March 6, 1982.

Portrait of Ayn, by Ilona R. S., 1965.

"I decided to be a writer, not in order to save the world nor to serve my fellowmen, but for the simple, personal, selfish, egotistical happiness of creating the kind of men and events I could like, respect and admire.

"You see, I am an atheist and I have only one religion: the sublime in human nature. There is nothing to approach the sanctity of the highest type of man possible, and there is nothing that gives me the same reverent feeling, the feeling when one's spirit wants to kneel, bare-headed. Do not call it hero-worship, because it is more than that."

"It is a kind of strange and improbable white-heat where admiration becomes religion, and religion becomes philosophy, and philosophy—the whole of one's life."

"My personal life is a postscript to my novels; it consists of the sentence 'And I mean it.' I have always lived by the philosophy I present in my books—and it has worked for me, as it works for my characters. The concretes differ, the abstractions are the same."

Ayn Rand waged a lifelong battle for reason and individualism. Like a ferocious angel, she fought.

Cover of Anthem, Signet paperback.

And beside her in the ranks—glowing from the tattered pages of books that have been read over and over again—are the men and women she created.

The characters who will forever fight for the same principles and the same sense of life.